In Celebration of Revised 780:

Music in the *Dewey Decimal Classification*

Edition 20

Compiled by Richard B. Wursten

MLA Technical Report No. 19

Music Library Association

1990

The Music Library Association

P.O. Box 487, Canton, MA 02021

"Appreciation of 780 Music, or, Left-Handed Bell Ringing," by Winton E. Matthews, Jr., published by permission of Forest Press/OCLC.
"Appendix: Two-Level Summary of 780, *DDC* 20" reprinted with permission of Forest Press/OCLC.
"Grand Messe des 780's (With Apologies to Berlioz)" by Russell Sweeney © 1990 by Russell Sweeney. All rights reserved. Published by permission of the author.

ISSN: 0094-5099

ISBN: 0-914954-42-3

MLA Technical Reports
Series Editor
Richard P. Smiraglia

Library of Congress Cataloging in Publication Data
In celebration of revised 780 : music in the Dewey Decimal
    Classification, edition 20 / compiled by Richard B. Wursten.
        p.   cm.—(MLA technical report ; no. 19)
    Includes bibliographical references.
    ISBN 0-914954-42-3
    1. Classification—Music. 2. Classification, Dewey decimal.
I. Wursten, Richard Bruce, 1938–   . II. Series.
ML 111.145 1990
025.4'678—dc20   90-40495
                                                       CIP
                                                       MN

Contents

CONTENTS

Introduction

by

Richard B. Wursten

From Proposed Revision to DDC 20:
A Brief History of the Revised 780 Music

The papers in this report principally are derived from a
program session that took place on March 16, 1989, at the Annual
Conference of the Music Library Association (MLA) in Cleveland,
Ohio.[1] In my Introduction to that session, I described the publication
of the 20th edition of the *Dewey Decimal Classification (DDC)*,[2]
"including a brand-new Phoenix schedule for 780 Music,"
as a major event in the world of music librarianship. In retrospect,
this statement is somewhat misleading, for the Phoenix schedule for
780 music can hardly be considered new; as of this writing, in fact, it
has existed in one form or another for almost fifteen years.

The history of the Phoenix schedule goes back to 1983, when, in
response to a query from Forest Press, the (British) Library
Association's Dewey Decimal Classification Subcommittee identified
780 Music as the Dewey class most urgently in need of revision.[3]
Shortly thereafter, the Press funded the establishment of a Project
Team headed by Russell Sweeney, then Principal Lecturer in the
Department of Librarianship, Leeds Polytechnic, to undertake the
necessary revisions. John P. Clews, who had completed graduate
degrees in Music and Librarianship from the University of Hull and
Leeds Polytechnic, respectively, was appointed Research Assistant,
and the project got underway in September, 1974.[4]

Richard B. Wursten is Director, Music Listening Center, and Adjunct Associate
Professor, University of North Carolina-Greensboro.

The Project Team was assisted by a Working Party on Music consisting of some of the most eminent librarians in England.[5] Sweeney explains:

> As each section of the proposed schedule was prepared, it was sent to the members of the Working Party, which held meetings in November 1974, January, March and June 1975. The meetings of the Working Party were of great value to the Project Team, offering a forum for the discussion of ideas presented in the early revisions, and criticism of proposals at all stages of the project.[6]

The first version of the revised classification was completed and presented to Forest Press in August, 1975. Over the next four years, it was tested and commented upon by numerous individuals and libraries, extensively revised in response to suggestions received, and finally approved for publication as a separate at a meeting of the Decimal Classification Editorial Policy Committee in April, 1979.[7] In 1980, it was published by Forest Press as *Proposed Revision of 780 Music (PR)*.[8]

As suggested elsewhere in this volume by Sweeney, Forest Press had originally entertained the idea of incorporating the *PR* and other Phoenix schedules into the 19th edition of *DDC*. As it happened, however, the 19th edition appeared with no major revisions in 780 Music, for the Decimal Classification Editorial Policy Committee decided to defer final acceptance of the *PR* until the music library profession had been given ample opportunity to pass judgment upon the new schedules.

> It was anticipated that the Press would receive a large number of comments from the music library profession, and that a decision to adopt the *PR* for inclusion in the 20th edition of Dewey in its present form, with further changes, or not at all would depend largely upon these comments. As reported in the Winter 1983 issue of *DC&*[9] the Decimal Classification Editorial Policy Committee recommended that a target date of December 31, 1984 be set for the receipt of comments from the profession, and that a firm decision concerning the future of the *PR* be made in 1985.[10]

Reactions to the new Phoenix schedule for 780 Music were not long in coming, and were for the most part overwhelmingly favorable. Reviews appeared in a number of journals,[11] and two major works on music librarianship. Brian Redfern's *Organizing Music in Libraries* (1978)[12] and E. T. Bryant's *Music Librarianship: A Practical Guide* (1985),[13] included sections on the new schedule. Two years before its publication in 1980, Redfern described the *PR* as "a remarkable achievement ..." that "succeeds in introducing the basic structure of the BCM [*British Catalogue of Music Classification*] [14] faceted scheme into the DC enumerative schedules without too great a wrench."[15] He touched briefly upon a number of its most noteworthy features, namely, its increased capacity for building faceted numbers through preestablished citation orders, creation of an option to make the composer the primary facet of music literature, and increased hospitality to classification of non-Western music and musical traditions such as jazz, folk, and popular music.[16] Bryant, writing some years later, also recognized the *PR*'s debt to the *BCM*. "At first glance," he wrote, "the possibility of expressing *BCM* classification in numerals and fitting the whole scheme into a decimal basis, so that the schedules occupy class 780, seems highly unlikely. Nevertheless, it has been done brilliantly ...."[17] By way of illustration, he showed how several complex concepts discussed in an earlier section on the *BCM* (for example, performance practice in Beethoven's piano sonatas) would be similarly constructed and expressed by faceted numbers in the *PR*.[18]

In 1982, the British Catalogue officially began using the *PR* to classify music and music literature.[19] A number of other large British and Australian libraries soon followed its lead, including those at Trinity College (Dublin), Trinity and All Saints College (Horsforth), Sydney Opera House (Sydney, Australia), La Trobe University (Bundoora, Victoria, Australia), and the City University of London. In the United States, the Stockton-San Joaquin County Public Library tested *PR* by using it to classify a small sample of sound recordings, books on music, and scores. In 1983, the Resources and Technical Services Division of the American Library Association (ALA) formed a subcommittee to study the *PR*.[20] After coming together at two ALA meetings–the Midwinter Meeting in

Washington, D. C. (January, 1984) and the Annual Conference in
Dallas, Texas (July, 1984)—this group submitted a list of proposed
changes to the DDC Editorial Policy Committee. Their comments,
along with those from other libraries and individuals, led to further
refinements in the *PR*, and the final version was submitted to Forest
Press in 1988 for inclusion in the 20th edition of *DDC*.

Criticisms of Dewey 780 Music:
A Mandate for Change

Ever since its first appearance as a 44-page pamphlet in
1876,[21] *DDC* has been used by more libraries than any other system
of classification. As Bryant wrote, "The Dewey scheme is probably
used in more libraries than all other schemes added together ...."[22]
This assertion is supported by Comaromi, who found that *DDC* is
used by 85.4% of all libraries in the United States and Canada,[23] and
by statistics in the Introduction to the 20th edition.[24]

In view of the immense popularity of *DDC* as a classification
tool for library collections in general, it might come as a surprise to
many to learn that one section of the schedules—780 Music—has
always been the subject of intense criticism both in Great Britain and
the United States. The Council of the *British National Bibliography*
found Dewey 780 Music so unsatisfactory, in fact, that music scores
were excluded from the *British National Bibliography* until the
appearance of E. J. Coates' draft outlines for the *British Catalogue of
Music Classification* in 1957, after which both music and music
literature were listed in a new publication, the *British Catalogue of
Music*.[25] Another early critic, Lionel McColvin, wrote that "Dewey's
music section, with its haphazard overclassification and the
confusion of music and musical literature, could scarcely be worse."[26]
McColvin was so dissatisfied with Dewey's scheme for Music, in fact,
that he devised his own system, totally rearranging the material in

780 Music, but retaining Dewey's numbers for the benefit of librarians who wished to substitute his arrangement for the Music section of Dewey.[27] As E. T. Bryant explained in his *Music Librarianship*, 2nd ed., "McColvin simply scrapped the *DDC* music schedules and replaced them with others which used the same numerical basis of 780 to 789."[28] Bryant was of the opinion, unquestionably shared by many music librarians, that "neither Melvil Dewey, despite his many virtues and abilities, nor his successors, seem to have had very much knowledge or appreciation of music."[29] While he admitted that each edition of 780 music was an improvement over the last, he nevertheless believed (prophetically, as it turned out) that "nothing less than a complete recasting of class 780 ..." would "bring it into line with modern ideas and needs."[30]

McColvin and Bryant were not alone in their dissatisfaction with Dewey 780 Music and its inability to keep abreast of new developments in music. "With the rich development of modern music as well as of music research in the last 70 years," maintained Kathi Meyer-Baer, "the use of the Decimal system has lead [sic] to such confusion that it seems proper to discuss its inconsistencies."[31] Gordon Stevenson wrote, "I'm afraid that many librarians have lived unhappily with Dewey's 780's ...."[32] Finally, Redfern wrote that the Dewey Decimal Classification "is the least satisfactory of all the schemes in its treatment of music."[33]

One of the principal deficiencies in previous editions of 780 Music, as Redfern and others recognized all too clearly, was its inability to adapt quickly to new musical forms, movements, innovations, and concepts. Figure 1, a comparison of the numbers for Piano music in the 11th (1922)[34] and 19th (1979)[35] editions, will suffice to show how few substantial changes took place over a period of almost 60 years. The 11th edition has no class numbers for keyboard string instruments other than the piano, and no numbers for such important forms as preludes, suites, fugues and other contrapuntal forms, and jazz. The 19th edition acknowledges, at least by implication, the existence of keyboard stringed instruments

Figure 1

Class numbers for Piano music, DDC 11

786.4   Piano music   General collections
For piano concerto, see 785.6

.41   Sonata   Sonatina   Rondo

.42   Fantasia   Arabesque

.43   Nocturne   Meditation   Romantic   Descriptiv
Songs without words

.44   March and march form   Polonaise Polka Mazurka

.45   Dance form: national, classic, idealized

.46   Modern dance music   Society, festiv

.47   Etudes   Artistic
For études for instruction see 786.3

.48   Variations, transcriptions

.49   Arrangements
Four hands and more; e.g. orchestral music arranged for
piano

Class numbers for Music for keyboard string
instruments, DDC 19

786.4   Music for keyboard string instruments
• • • • • • • • • • • • • • • • • • •
Class comprehensive works in 786.4

.41   *Sonatas, sonatinas, rondos

.42   *Fantasias, fugues, rhapsodies, arabesques

.43   Romantic and descriptive music
Examples: nocturnes, meditations, ballads, songs without
words

.44   *Marches, polonaises, polkas, mazurkas
*Add as instructed under 786.41-786.49

.45   *Dances
Including national, classic, idealized dances; dance suites,
square dance music
*For polonaises, polkas, mazurkas, see 786.44; modern
dance music, 786.46*

.46   *Modern dance music
         Examples: ballroom dance music, jazz music.

.47   *Artistic études

.48   *Variations and suites

.49   Music for more than one performer
         Not provided for in 786.41-786.48

---

in addition to the piano, and adds most of the forms missing in the
11th edition. There are still no numbers, however, for preludes or for
more recent developments, such as dodecaphony and aleatory music,
and jazz sneaks in almost unnoticed under Modern dance music.
Neither edition shows any awareness of the fact that arrangements
exist for one pianist as well as two or more. In the 11th edition,
arrangements are followed by the note "Four hands and more ...;"[36]
in the 19th, they are found under 786.49, "Music for more than one
performer."[37]

Redfern attributed *DDC*'s resistance to change largely to its
very popularity. He wrote:

> Because of so many large libraries now using DC, there is a great
> burden of feeling against change, even in the way the schedules of
> the scheme are revised to take account of modern knowledge and
> classification theory. This means that a reader using a number of
> libraries, all classified by Dewey, may well find that each uses a
> different edition of the schedules.[38]

Bryant noted that many librarians, when faced with a new
edition of Dewey, "are likely to continue with the edition already in
use, simply because of the labour involved in reclassifying and
amending the class marks on the spines of books and scores ...."[39]
Even when *DDC* users adopt new editions, discovered Comaromi,
they often try to avoid reclassifying materials. "Upon acceptance of a
new edition or new numbers developed and assigned between
editions, at least two-thirds of all *DDC* users do *no* reclassing when
subjects have been relocated."[40] This actually happened in the

university library in which I was formerly employed as a music cataloger; when the cataloging department officially adopted the 19th edition, 18th edition numbers already in use were written into the schedules in place of many of the new class numbers.

No less perplexing a problem than 780 Music's inability to stay abreast of new developments in music and music classification was its failure to create a satisfactory distinction, as do McColvin, *Library of Congress Classification (LCC)*, and *BCM*, between music and music literature. For the first forty-six years of its existence, *DDC* made no attempt whatsoever to separate music from works about music, as is evident from the following note in the 11th edition: "All heds include the music itself and everything about it: score, libretto, history, criticism, etc."[41] The 12th edition was the first to acknowledge the difference between music and music literature; it retained the note just quoted, but added "if preferd, the music itself may be separated from the works about it by prefixing to its class numbers an M, with MS for sheet music."[42] (One wonders precisely what was meant by sheet music, and how it differed from other scores.)

The note thus expanded was repeated without change in the 13th and 14th editions, but reduced to one sentence in the 15th, as follows: "Music may be separated from works about music by prefixing M to [the] class number."[43] In the 16th edition, it was enlarged to two paragraphs, each offering a different option for distinguishing music from works about music.

> Use separate numbers for music itself (scores and parts), where provided, to separate it from works about music, e.g., works about violin and violin music 787.1-787.12, violin music itself 787.15 .... If preferred class scores and works about music in the same number, distinguishing scores by prefixing M to the number, e.g., works about violin and violin music 787.1, violin music itself M787.1.[44]

The 17th, 18th, and 19th editions included a similar note, but expanded the digits added to distinguish scores and parts from .15 to .151-.154 (for individual composers, collections by more than one composer, and miniature scores, respectively).[45]

Although the Project Team clearly recognized the need to resolve this problem once and for all, they stopped far short of the ultimate solution, i.e., the creation of separate sequences of numbers for music and music literature as in McColvin, *LCC*, and *BCM*. They elected, in fact, to retain the two options already established in earlier editions, but as Sweeney explained in Autumn 1976, to give preference to M, thus creating a mnemonic relationship between music and works about music.

> Rather than divide the available notation 780-789 into two sequences as in McColvin's substitution ... we are proposing that the distinction between scores and literature should be made by prefixing an alphabetical symbol, e.g. M to the class number for scores. This device is already available as an option in DC 18th edition–our proposal would make this the first choice. The device immediately ensures a mnemonic relationship between scores and literature.
>
> 786.2   A book about the piano
>
> M786.2   Music for the piano.[46]

For unknown reasons, concessions seem to have been made at some later date, for neither the *PR* nor *DDC* 20 expresses an unmistakable preference for the use of M to distinguish scores from literature. The 20th edition, for example, offers two choices which are not significantly different from those found in most earlier editions:

> Option: Distinguish scores by prefixing a letter or other symbol to the number for treatises, e.g., music for violin M787.2 or &787.2, and distinguish miniature scores from other scores by a special prefix, e.g., MM787.2; distinguish recordings in a similar manner, e.g., violin recordings R787.2 or MR787.2. *Alternatively* distinguis scores, texts, recordings by adding to the number for treatises the numbers following 78 in 780.26-780.269, e.g., miniature scores of music for violin 787.20265.[47]

In witnessing the revised 780 Music's inability to come up with a solution to this problem that eliminates forever the ambiguities found in earlier editions, one is reminded of the old French proverb, "Plus ça change, plus c'est la même chose" (The more things change, the more they stay the same"). It is unfortunate that so much effort should have been expended upon an issue for which a perfectly adequate solution had already been proposed, in the 15th edition of *DDC*,[48] as far back as 1951. Perhaps future editions of Dewey 780 Music will come to share this writer's belief that the use of one appropriate symbol at the beginnings of class numbers (M for scores, MM for miniature scores, R for sound recordings, V or T for videotapes, and so on) is the *one and only* device needed to separate music from works about music. This perfectly simple procedure has two immediate advantages over all others: it creates, as already explained, a useful mnemonic relationship between scores (miniature scores, sound recordings, videotapes) and literature, and eliminates the necessity for fussing with one more set of added digits at the end of class numbers, thus allowing the cataloger to move on quickly to more demanding classification problems.

While the issues just discussed are certainly not insubstantial, they pale into insignificance when one turns to a closer examination of the class numbers themselves. Redfern's description of the 781 section as "a hotch-potch"[49] could be applied without reservations to the entire Music division. Most subjects are analyzed in far too little detail, so that catalogers more often than not are forced to settle for approximations. A host of significant topics and concepts do not appear at all (see Figure 1), and many of those that do occur are to be found in totally illogical places or scattered willy-nilly all over the schedules. And, as almost every critic of Dewey has remarked, far too little provision is made for non-classical traditions of music such as jazz, popular music, and folk music, or for non-Western musics of any description. Liturgical music of non-Christian religions, for example, is represented in the 19th edition by one number, 783.209 (to which may be added the number for a specific religion, e.g., Buddhism from 292-299).[50]

A few examples from the 19th edition will serve to illustrate the problems identified above. To begin with, the entire universe of "General principles and considerations" at 781 (those items described

in Phoenix 780 Music as elements, techniques, character and
traditions, and musical forms) is represented by a total of 45 numbers
(as compared to over 200 in Phoenix 780). 781.4 is subdivided into
two topics that most thinking musicians would probably regard as
strange bedfellows indeed, namely, Melody at 781.41 and
Counterpoint at 781.42 (DDC 20 places Counterpoint under Texture,
along with four related topics–Monody, Heterophony, Polyphony,
and Homophony–that have no place at all in previous editions of
DDC). Musical forms at 781.5 consists of exactly four subdivisions
(Sonata, Dance music, Program music, and Jazz and related forms),
at least two of which most musicians would not hold for musical
forms at all. Jazz, at 781.57, is distinguished by a total of three
subdivisions (Ragtime, Blues, and Hot jazz and swing), while Popular
songs at 784.5 fares little better with only four: Country music,
Blues, Rock (Rock 'n' Roll), and Soul. The last-named example drew
a particularly caustic response from Sanford Berman:

> Public libraries, in particular, have for years been ill-served by
> Dewey music schedules that allocate a *single* notation for "Popular
> music." That sole number, presumably, is sufficient to accommodate
> thousands of records and tapes in genres as diverse as Blues, Rock,
> Country, and Soul. Well, it *doesn't* accomodate [sic] them.[51]

Needless to say, such examples are replicated on many pages of the
schedules for Music.

Of the numerous illogical subject sequences found in the 19th
edition, only two need be mentioned here. The first of these, to which
Redfern drew particular attention,[52] is a sequence of four topics
whose relationship to one another defies any sort of conventional
wisdom: Embellishments at 781.67, Music of ethnic groups and
various specific countries and localities at 781.7, and other topics at
781.9, subdivided into Musical instruments (.91) and Words to be
sung or recited with music (.96)! The second is a sequence beginning
at 785.1, reproduced in Figure 2 without the various explanatory
notes and the subdivisions under Chamber music.[53] Virtually no

Figure 2

Class numbers for Instrumental ensembles and their music, *DDC* **19**

785.1   Symphonies and Band music

.11	Symphonies for orchestra
.12	Band music
.13	Military band music
.2	Music for orchestra with incidental vocal parts
.3	Miscellaneous music for orchestra
.31	Romantic music
.32	Program music
.34	Variations and other large works
.4	Music for small ensembles
.41	Dance music
.42	Jazz
.43	Music for rhythm and percussion bands
.5	Independent overtures for orchestra
.6	Concertos
.7	Chamber music
.8	Suites for orchestra

thought seems to have been given to this arrangement of performing groups and musical forms. Music for orchestra is split into four separate segments by the interpolation first of band music, then of small ensembles and jazz, and finally of chamber music. Jazz is inserted between orchestral variations and overtures, while chamber music intrudes, almost as an afterthought, between concertos and suites for orchestra (in *DDC* 20 780 Music, the entire 785 section is allotted to chamber music). No clue is given as to what is meant by "other large works" (785.34) or "small ensembles" (785.4). Redfern suggested rearranging the entire section, first by *kind* of ensemble and then by form, as follows:[54]

785 .1	Orchestras and their music
.11	Symphonies
.12	Symphonic poems
.13	Variations
.14	Suites
.15	Concertos
785 .2	Bands
.21	Symphonies
.22/3	Variations
.26	Dance Music
.27	Jazz

etc.

Of the many topics that cause endless confusion and irritation by being scattered needlessly throughout the schedules, jazz is among the most frequently mentioned. Jazz and related forms are found at 781.57-.574, 784.53 (Blues), 785.0666-.0667 (Dance orchestra and jazz orchestra), 785.0672 (Jazz band), 785.42 (Music for small ensembles), and 786.46 (Under modern dance music for keyboard instrument, along with ballroom dance music!). As is far too often the case, this apparent wealth of numbers actually conceals a lack of provision for numerous situations. Where does one class jazz for a solo instrument such as saxophone, for example, or jazz vocals with piano or other accompaniment? What about jazz piano music that can hardly be described as "Modern dance music," such as that of Tatum, Garner, or Brubeck? Finally, how does one treat the music of pivotal figures such as Basie or Ellington, which often cuts across the boundaries between two or more categories (putting it another way, at what point does a small jazz ensemble become a jazz band or jazz orchestra?)?

Another example of scattering that has provoked no end of adverse criticism is *DDC*'s treatment of music biography. In this

area, as in that of music versus music literature, it appears that the
editors of successive editions of *DDC* have simply been incapable of
settling upon one course of action. In earlier editions, 927.8 was the
preferred location for musicians' biographies. The 16th edition
retained this number, but also provided another, 780.92, for criticism
and appraisal of individual musicians. In characteristic fashion,
however, 780 Music continued to hem and haw; it seems that two
numbers were still not enough. As Bryant explained, it was
suggested:

> that biographies should be placed here [780.92] only if the library
> classed biography by subject, rather than placing all examples in
> class 920 and, further, that a subject approach be preferred for
> "individual musicians working in one medium" and offering, as an
> example, 787.1081 as the suggested symbol for a book dealing with
> an individual violinist.[55]

Later editions exacerbated the situation by offering still more class
numbers for musical biography. The 19th, for example, has at least
eight: in addition to the general location at 780.92, there are
numbers for persons associated with dramatic music (780.92), opera
(782.1092), sacred music (783.092), voice and vocal music (784.092),
instrumental ensembles (785.092), keyboard string instruments
(786.1092), and individual instruments under 786-789—in short, for
almost everyone except organists! As one writer pointed out:

> To split the literature in this way only places an additional obstacle
> in the library user's path, forces the cataloger into numerous time-
> consuming value judgments (whether, for example, a given
> monograph places more emphasis on Mahler as composer or as
> conductor), and will lead to split files for many musicians, e.g.,
> Mahler as composer (in 780.92) or as conductor (in 785.092).[56]

The *PR* came up with a novel solution, based largely upon the
model established by Coates' *British Catalogue of Music
Classification*, for this problem: it established the composer (but not
other musicians, such as performers or arrangers) as the primary
facet in literature about music, then set aside class 789 for individual
composers. 780.92 was kept for "Persons associated with music," but

followed by the note "Class individual composers in 789."[57]
Composers were assigned unique numbers from one of two tables, a
"Chronological list of composers" and an "Alphabetical list of
composers."[58] Each list provided three types of notation: numerical,
alphanumerical, and alphabetical. Using the Alphabetical list of
composers, for example, one would choose either 789.576, 789.034, or
789.OCK for Ockeghem; using the Chronological list, one would
place Ockeghem at 789.2 (1450-1599), then add from one of the three
options to create either 789.2'66, 789.2'034, or 789.2'OCK.
Composers not represented in the tables were to be classed either in
789 without further subdivision (Alphabetical list) or under "the
period in which the composer's first composition appeared or was
performed" (Chronological list).[59] Dunstable, for example, would be
classed at 789.1 (To 1449) in the latter case.

As has been explained in detail elsewhere,[60] this scheme
presented far more formidable difficulties than those it was meant to
replace. To begin with, the two lists of composers—each containing
the same 307 names—included only those represented (as of 1975) by
at least five monographs in the Library of Congress. In theory, this
seems a sound enough criterion; in actual practice, it resulted in the
provision of specific numbers for world-class figures such as
Balanchivadze, Peter Frampton, Vardapest Komitas, and Rantarō
Taki, while many vastly more important composers such as Landini,
Dunstable, Obrecht, Isaac, Böhm, Johann Stamitz, Hummel,
Sessions, and Elliott Carter, to mention just a few, were left in
"standing room." In the second place, the possible combinations of
two lists and three methods for formulating composers' class
numbers would have led to complexities of absolutely awesome
dimensions. Use of the Alphabetical list, for example, would have
created two sequences of names, one for those with unique numbers
and one for those without, thus forcing the librarian or patron who
went directly to the shelf for material on a given composer to look in
both places. Use of the Chronological list would have resulted in
twelve sequences of names on the shelf: one under the general

numbers and one under the assigned numbers for each of the six chronological subdivisions!

The composers' lists evidently engendered a barrage of negative comments from the library profession, for they were dropped from the *PR* before its publication in *DDC* 20. 789 was retained as an optional location for literature about composers but not officially adopted by the 20th edition. In the "Third Summary: The Thousand Sections" (Volume 2), it is printed as an empty number.[61] It is not listed at all in the summary at the beginning of 780 Music,[62] but appears in parentheses at the end of the Music schedules, where one is given the option of using it for treatises on composers (789), traditions of music (789.1), or both.[63]

Thus 780 Music once more is reduced to two simple numbers for musicians' biographies, 780.92 and 789 (for those who choose to separate literature about composers from literature about other musicians), with individuals classed under each number to be distinguished by a cutter number or some other alphabetizing device. One would think these two numbers perfectly adequate for all needs; unfortunately, old habits die hard. An example from the 20th edition *Manual for the Dewey Decimal Classification* gives 787.4092 as the class number for a biography of Pablo Casals (from 787.4 for cello and 780.92 for performers).[64] One can only hope that the editors of *DDC* will someday make up their minds, once and for all, that a biography of Casals is not a treatise on cello music, despite the fact that Casals was a great cellist, and class such a work accordingly, i.e., under 780.92. Since we now know that Casals was a composer as well as a cellist and conductor, his biography could actually be classed in either 780.92 or 789 (which points up all the more strongly the folly of trying to separate literature about composers from literature about "other musicians").

Perhaps the most serious weakness in earlier editions of 780 Music was the creation of a great many fixed class relationships between independent characteristics, e.g., executants and forms, through the use of what might be described as precoordinate numbers. The 19th edition, for example, has specific numbers for orchestral variations (785.34) and variations for piano (786.48), but none for other executants. One can classify a sonata for keyboard stringed instrument (786.41), or an organ sonata (786.81), but not a sonata for violin, trumpet, or clarinet, for the simple reason that there are no sonata numbers for the latter three instruments. There is a number for pedal studies for piano (786.35) but, curiously enough, none for organ; the latter must be classed in 786.73, the general number for organ studies and exercises. One can precisely classify organ preludes (786.83) but not one of the most important genres for organ, chorale preludes. In each of the above cases, the lack of any apparatus, aside from standard subdivisions, for the synthesis of two or more independent characteristics makes it impossible to assign class numbers to any compounds not already specified in the schedules. There is no way, for example, to combine the number for trombone (787.2) with the number for sonata forms (781.52) so as to create a class number for a trombone sonata.

As the reader probably is aware by now, 780 Music in *DDC* 20 largely eliminates the aforementioned problems by creating, for the first time in the history of *DDC*, a totally faceted scheme, modeled principally on the *BCM*. Since this scheme is explained fully in two of the following papers, it will be summarized as briefly as possible at this point. To begin with, the architects of the new schedule have organized the subject material of music into a sequence of clearly-defined facets. For music scores, this sequence begins with the executant, i.e., the performer(s), as the primary facet; for literature about music, it begins with the composer (for librarians who choose to class literature about composers in 789). Secondly, the schedules have been vastly reorganized, so that whatever comes first in the schedules appears last in the citation order: standard subdivisions are in 780; basic principles, elements, techniques, character, and forms in 781; executants in 782-788; and composers in 789. To create any faceted number, therefore, one simply proceeds in reverse citation order, starting with the element appearing last in the schedules and working toward the beginning (there are a few exceptions to this principle, one of which will be illustrated in the following paragraph). For example, the class number for a trombone sonata (788.93'183) is formed by starting with the number for trombone (788.93), then adding -183 from 784.183 (Sonata forms). The number for counterpoint in trombone sonatas (788.93'183'1286) is arrived at by the same process: to the number for trombone, one first adds -183 as already explained, then -1286 from 781.286 (Counterpoint).

One final example will serve to show the superiority of the new faceted scheme over all previous editions of 780 Music. Earlier editions contained only one number for works for solo instrument(s) and accompanying ensemble, thus making it impossible for the cataloger to distinguish between works by types of executants or to differentiate between concertos and other types of works for solo instrument(s) and accompanying ensemble. In *DDC* 20, 780 Music eliminates these problems by providing: 1) separate numbers for Concertos and other instrumental forms at 784.182-.189; and 2) a range of new numbers (784.22-.28) for Orchestra with vocal parts and Orchestra with one or more featured solo instruments. This scheme allows one to specify both solo instrument(s) and musical form, and thus to precisely classify works as diverse as a concerto for piano and orchestra (784.262), the Franck *Symphonic Variations* for piano and orchestra (784.262'1825), or the Mozart *Sinfonie Concertante* for violin, viola and orchestra (784.24'1845). In addition, special provision is made for the classification of works for solo instrument(s) and ensembles other than full orchestra. Following the instructions given under 784.2-.9, one can thus construct a number for a rondo for oboe and wind band (784.8'0824'1852) by starting with 784.8 (Wind band), then adding -0824 (from 781.824, Rondo forms) and -1852 (from 788.52, Oboe). This example illustrates one of a few previously-mentioned exceptions in 780 Music in which synthesis does not proceed strictly in reverse citation order; in this case, the number for form is added before that for the solo instrument.

This Introduction has dealt principally with several significant problems found in earlier editions of *DDC* 780 Music and their solutions in *DDC* 20, largely through a complete reorganization

of the Music schedules and the creation for the first time of a truly
faceted scheme of class numbers. It must be remembered, however,
that the capacity for building synthesized numbers of any desired
length and specificity is but one of several significant innovations in
DDC 20's schedule for Music. Other important innovations, all of
which will be the subject of more extensive discussions in the papers
that follow, include: 1) the use of the Sachs-Hornbostel fourfold
classification of musical instruments[65] as a basis for the
subarrangement of instruments in 786-788, thus making the
schedules much more hospitable to non-Western instruments and
their music; 2) a new section at 781.6, entitled "Traditions of music
and specific kinds of music," in which is found a large array of
numbers for folk and popular music (both Western and non-
Western), jazz, non-Western art music, Western art ("classical")
music (for those who wish to treat classical music as only one of
several traditions), and specific kinds of music, such as sacred music
and music to accompany customary actions and stages of life cycle;
and, 3) the provision of an optional number, 789, for those who choose
to limit 781-788 to one tradition, such as Western classical music,
and to class all other traditions in this number.

 While it is evident that some important problems have yet to
be satisfactorily resolved, 780 Music in *DDC* 20 remains nonetheless
a truly impressive achievement, and one that merits the attention of
music librarians everywhere. One could wish that Dewey and non-
Dewey librarians alike might fall upon it with great shouts of joy and
begin using it immediately to classify or reclassify their collections.
Unfortunately, this is unlikely to happen, for initial enthusiasm for
the new schedule must soon be tempered by the realization that a
large number of practical issues must be addressed and solved before
its widespread adoption can become a reality. These issues will
occupy a prominent place in the last two papers in this volume.

Contributors to This Volume

This volume contains the first published collection of writings on the revised schedule for Music in *DDC* 20. All of the papers published here are by recognized authorities in the field of classification, and thus represent a significant contribution to the growing body of critical literature on the new schedule. Taken as a group, the papers deal with five distinct aspects of the revised 780: its historical background and conception, its physical characteristics and practical applications, its potential as a tool for online subject retrieval, the probable effects of its adoption upon the music literature collections of a large university library, and its implications for public libraries and public library music collections. The first four papers were presented at the MLA session described earlier, while the fifth was read, under a different title,[66] at the Annual Conference of the American Library Association in Dallas, Texas in June, 1989.

Russell Sweeney, head of the Department of Library and Information Studies at Leeds Polytechnic, Leeds, England, was the chief architect of the Phoenix schedule and principal author of the *PR*. He was the editor of *Catalogue & Index* from 1973 to 1980. Since 1981, he has served as both chairman of the Library Association Dewey Decimal Classification Committee and Library Association representative to the *DDC* Editorial Policy Committee. In addition to the *PR*, Sweeney's publications include reviews and articles in *Catalogue & Index, Brio, The Journal of Documentation*, and *Library Resources & Technical Services*. In "Grand Messe des 780's (With Apologies to Berlioz)," he explains why a large-scale revision of 780 Music was felt to be essential, and outlines the mechanisms through which the revision was carried out. He identifies the main problems that had to be addressed in creating a new schedule, and explains how each of these was dealt with in the revised 780. Finally, he discusses the changes that took place, principally in response to comments from the library profession, at each step along the way from the presentation of the original report to Forest Press in 1975 to the publication of *DDC* 20 in 1989. Especially helpful for an understanding of these changes are summaries of 780 Music in both the *PR* and *DDC* 20.

Winton E. Matthews, Jr., has been at the Library of Congress since 1967, first in the Subject Cataloging Division and then in the Decimal Classification Division. He became an assistant editor in the Decimal Classification Division on April 1, 1985. Matthews was an assistant author for two Forest Press publications, the *PR* (1980) and the *Manual on the Use of Dewey Decimal Classification: Edition 19* (1982), and is one of the editors of *DDC* 20. His paper, "Appreciation of 780 Music, or, Left-handed Bell Ringing," describes the new 780 schedule, beginning with an overall view of each of the four major sections (Generalities, Vocal music, Instrumental music, and Optional provision for treatises on composers and traditions of music). With the help of four detailed examples (Music for Baptist weddings, Music of opera vs. staging operas, Harmony in piano sonatas, and Recording of trumpet music), Matthews then gives explicit instructions for using the revised schedule to create complex synthesized class numbers.

Arnold S. Wajenberg, professor and principal cataloger at the University of Illinois at Urbana-Champaign, has been a visiting professor of cataloging in the library schools at the University of Illinois at Urbana-Champaign, University of Chicago, and University of California, Los Angeles. He is currently a member of the DDC Editorial Policy Committee. Wajenberg is the author or co-author of three published cataloging manuals, numerous articles in journals such as *Illinois Libraries, Law Library Journal,* and *Journal of Library Automation,* and the entries on cataloging and classification (with Michael Gorman) in the 1986 and 1987 volumes of the *ALA Yearbook of Library and Information Services.* In 1983, he published an article in *Information Technology and Libraries,* "MARC Coding of DDC for Subject Retrieval,"[67] in which he showed how the unused second indicator values of MARC tags 082 and 092, together with additional subfields for these tags, could be utilized to encode hierarchical relationships among class numbers, thus facilitating subject retrieval in an online catalog. Wajenberg's contribution to this publication, "Online Subject Retrieval Using the New Schedule," explains how his scheme can be applied to the revised schedule for 780 Music, thus making it possible for an online catalog to retrieve not only material classed in general numbers such as 780 and 781, but also material classed in much more specific synthesized numbers.

Charles Forrest is director of Instructional Support Services in the Candler Library at Emory University, Atlanta, Georgia. Prior to assuming this position, he was assistant professor and undergraduate librarian and media coordinator at the University of Illinois at Urbana-Champaign. Forrest has published articles on a variety of topics, is active on several ALA committees, and has made presentations at conferences of the American Library Association, Library Information and Technology Association, and other organizations.

Richard P. Smiraglia, the editor of *MLA Technical Reports*, is senior lecturer in the School of Library Service, Columbia University, and former associate professor and music catalog librarian at the University of Illinois at Urbana-Champaign. He has authored three books, co-authored or edited five others, and published a large number of journal articles. Smiraglia is a very active member of the Music Library Association; he has chaired several committees in this organization, has been the MLA Representative to and later chair of ALA's Committee on Cataloging: Description and Access, and served a two-year term (1986-88) on MLA's Board of Directors. The paper published here, "Radical Change with Minimal Disruption: The Effect of Revised 780 Music on the University of Illinois Library Shelf Arrangement," chronicles the results of a study initiated by Smiraglia and Forrest at the University of Illinois at Urbana-Champaign. The authors set out to "assess the impact of the *Proposed Revision* on shelf arrangement of books about music in the University of Illinois Library ...." A carefully-controlled sample of music monographs was retrieved, and surrogates were then reclassified using the *PR*. Material classified before December 1980 was also reclassified in *DDC* 19, so that the study would compare only class numbers in the 19th edition and the *PR*. The information retrieved was used to answer four basic questions relating to changes and their impact on shelf arrangement, and the resulting conclusions were surprisingly favorable for those contemplating the adoption of the revised schedule for general collections of books about music.

Pat Thoms has been head cataloger at the Stockton-San Joaquin County Public Library for over fourteen years. She is a past chair of ALA's Committee on Cataloging: Description and Access, and is currently a member of the *DDC* Editorial Policy Committee and the Public Library Association's Cataloging Needs of Public Libraries Committee. She has read papers at meetings of the American Library Association and American Association of School Librarians. In "A Music Muddle? *DDC* 20 in the Public Library," Thomas develops three themes: 1) "The public library is, by definition, a general library"; 2) "*DDC* has traditionally been a classification system for everyman"; and, 3) "The revised schedule ... is a scheme best suited to classify a predetermined collection with known emphasis or bias ... [and] is not meant for everyman's music collection ...." Against this background, she identifies a number of problems that public libraries will have to face if the revised 780 is adopted, then presents some sugggestions for coping from her own experiences and those of other public librarians with whom she has spoken. Finally, Thomas echoes an idea introduced earlier in this Introduction: she implies very strongly that the keepers of many smaller, less specialized collections (i.e., the vast majority of those who use *DDC*) become accustomed to Dewey's "simplicity for the classifier" and "uniformity across the schedules as a whole," and might, as a result, become highly resistant to innovations such as those found in the schedule for Music.

Thomas's concluding remarks lead naturally to a final, highly provocative question: will Dewey catalogers long accustomed to time-honored ways of doing things find it difficult to modify their thinking, and thus become one of the biggest stumbling blocks in the path of a widespread acceptance of the revised 780 Music? Only time will tell.

Notes

1.   "The Dewey Decimal Classification Phoenix Schedule 780: A New Tool for Classification and Online Retrieval," session presented at the 58th Annual Conference of the Music Library Association, Cleveland, Ohio, March 16, 1989.

2.   Melvil Dewey, *Dewey Decimal Classification and Relative Index*, 20th ed., ed. John P. Comaromi et al. (Albany, N.Y.: Forest Press, 1989).

3.   *Proposed Revision of 780 Music: Based on Dewey Decimal Classification and Relative Index*, prepared under the direction of Russell Sweeney and John Clews (Albany, N.Y.: Forest Press, 1980).

4.   Russell Sweeney, "Music in the Dewey Decimal Classification," *Catalogue & Index*, no. 42 (Autumn 1976): 4.

5.   *Proposed Revision*, xi.

6.   Ibid.

7.   Ibid., viii.

8.   Ibid.

9.   "Guidelines to Users for Reactions to the *Proposed Revision of 780 Music*," *DC&* 4 (Oct. 1981): 8-10.

10.   Richard B. Wursten, "Review of Proposed Revision of 780 Music," *Cataloging & Classification Quarterly* 5, no. 2 (Winter 1984): 57.

11.   For a list of reviews of the *PR*, see Sweeney's paper, elsewhere in this volume.

12.   Brian Redfern, *Arrangement and Classification*, vol. 1 of *Organising Music in Libraries*, rev. ed. (London: Clive Bingley, 1978), 55-61.

13. Eric T. Bryant and Guy A. Marco, *Music Librarianship: A Practical Guide*, 2d ed. (Metuchen, N.J.: Scarecrow Press, 1985), 257-60.

14. E. J. Coates, comp., *British Catalogue of Music Classification* (London: British National Bibliography, 1960).

15. Redfern, *Arrangement*, 58.

16. Ibid.

17. Bryant and Marco, *Music Librarianship*, 257.

18. Ibid., 257-60.

19. *British Catalogue of Music: 1982* (London: The British Library, Bibliographic Services Division, 1983), vi.

20. Members of the Subcommittee were Frances Hinton (Chair), Richard B. Wursten, and Pat Thomas.

21. Melvil Dewey, *A Classification and Subject Index for Cataloguing and Arranging the Books and Pamphlets of a Library* (Amherst, Mass., 1876).

22. Eric T. Bryant, *Music Librarianship: A Practical Guide* (London: James Clarke & Co., 1959), 143.

23. John P. Comaromi, "Dewey in the USA & Canada," *Catalogue & Index* no. 43 (Winter 1976): 3.

24. *DDC*, 20th ed., vol. 1, xxvi.

25. *British Catalogue of Music*, (London: The Council of the British National Bibliography, 1957-   ).

26. Lionel R. McColvin and Harold Reeves, *Music Libraries: Their Organization and Contents, with a Bibliography of Music and Musical Literature*, vol. 1 (London: Grafton, 1937), 25.

27. Ibid., 27-39. According to Sweeney, a great many British librarians did adopt McColvin's scheme.

28. Bryant and Marco, *Music Librarianship*, 234.

29. Ibid., 215.

30. Ibid., 223.

31. Kathi Meyer-Baer, "Classifications in American Libraries," in *Reader in Music Librarianship*, ed. Carol June Bradley (Washington, D.C.: Microcard Editions, 1973), 172.

32. Gordon Stevenson, "Classification Chaos," in *Reader in Music Librarianship*, ed. Carol June Bradley (Washington, D.C.: Microcard Editions, 1973), 277.

33. Redfern, *Arrangement*, 55.

34. Melvil Dewey, *Decimal Classification and Relativ Index ...*, 11th ed., revized and enlarjd (Lake Placid Club, Adirondaks, N.Y.: Forest Pres, 1922), 780 Music (there are no page numbers in this ed.). Curious spellings in this and other Dewey citations are Melvil Dewey's own.

35. Idem., *Dewey Decimal Classification and Relative Index*, 19th ed., ed. Benjamin A. Custer (Albany, N.Y.: Forest Press, 1979), 2:1348-49.

36. Dewey, *Decimal Classification*, 11th ed., 780 Music.

37. Dewey, *Dewey Decimal Classification*, 19th ed., 2:1349.

38. Redfern, *Arrangement*, 55.

39. Bryant and Marco, *Music Librarianship*, 223.

40. Comaromi, "Dewey in the USA & Canada," 3.

41. Dewey, *Decimal Classification*, 11th ed., 780 Music.

42. Melvil Dewey, *Decimal Classification and Relativ Index...*, 12th ed., revized and enlarjd under direction of Dorcas Fellows (Lake Placid Club, Essex, N.Y.: Forest Pres, 1927), 780 Music (there are no page numbers in this ed.).

43. Idem., Dewey, *Decimal Classification and Relativ Index*, 15th ed., (Lake Placid Club, N.Y.: Forest Press, 1951), 382.

44. Idem., Dewey, *Decimal Classification and Relative Index*, 16th ed., (Lake Placid Club, Essex Co., N.Y.: Forest Press, 1958), 1:973.

45. Dewey, *Dewey Decimal Classification*, 19th ed., 2:1317.

46. Sweeney, "Music in the Dewey Decimal Classification," 4.

47. Dewey, *Dewey Decimal Classification*, 20th ed., 3:548; italics mine.

48. Dewey, *Dewey Decimal Classification*, 15th ed.,382.

49. Redfern, *Arrangement*, 56.

50 Dewey, *Dewey Decimal Classification*, 19th ed., 2:1329.

51. Sanford Berman, *HCL Cataloging Bulletin*, no. 36 (Sept./Oct. 1978): 37.

52. Redfern, *Arrangement*, 57.

53. Dewey, *Dewey Decimal Classification*, 19th ed., 2:1342-45.

54. Redfern, *Arrangement*, 58.

55. Bryant and Marco, *Music Librarianship*, 217.

56. Wursten, "Review of Proposed Revision," 65.

57. *Proposed Revision*, 5.

58. Ibid., 48-66.

59. Ibid., 49.

60. Wursten, "Review of Proposed Revision," 64-65.

61. Dewey, *Dewey Decimal Classification*, 20th ed., 2:xviii.

62. Ibid., 3:550.

63. Ibid., 3:599.

64. Ibid., 4:936.

65. Erich M. von Hornbostel and Curt Sachs, "Classification of Musical Instruments," trans. Anthony Baines and Klaus P. Wachsmann, *Galpin Society Journal* 14 (1961): 3-29.

66. Patricia M. Thomas, "Music in the Public Library," paper presented at the American Library Association Annual Conference, Dallas, Texas, June 27, 1989.

67. Arnold S. Wajenberg, "MARC Coding of DDC for Subject Retrieval," *Information Technology and Libraries* 2 (1983): 246-251.

Grand Messe des 780's
(With apologies to Berlioz)

by

Russell Sweeney

ABSTRACT: States the reasons for the perceived necessity for the revision of 780. Outlines the mechanisms for the progress of the revision and explores the various possibilities of a model for the revised schedules. Identifies the main problem areas which needed to be addressed in the revision and reviews the concepts and structures in the revised schedules. Considers the development and amendments to the proposed revision following the presentation of the report to the Forest Press and DCEPC in 1975 up to the publication of *The Proposed Revision...*, in 1980. Outlines the amendments made to *The Proposed Revision...*, in light of the comments from the profession up to the final decisions for inclusion of the schedules in ed. 20 of *DDC*.

Background

Soon after publication of Ed.18 of the *Dewey Decimal Classification (DDC)* in 1971, the (British) Library Association Dewey Decimal Classification Committee (LADDCC) were asked by the then Executive Director of Forest Press (publishers of *DDC*, since 1988 a division of OCLC) to suggest schedules which they believed should be considered for "Phoenix" revision in edition 19. After discussions on various contenders, the Committee agreed that top priority should be given to 780 Music. The main reasons for this choice were that the schedules were considered to be very unsatisfactory by many librarians, failing to make a distinction between music and music literature. This led many British librarians to reject the Dewey Decimal Classification (*DDC*) for the arrangement of music altogether and adopt McColvin's modification of *DDC*.[1] Other reasons were the

---

Russell Sweeney is Head, Department of Library and Information Studies, Leeds Polytechnic, England.

unsatisfactory treatment accorded to traditions of music other than the European Art tradition, and the exclusion of music from the British National Bibliography because of the poor arrangements in the class in DDC. The suggestion was accompanied by some broad ideas on the shape of any revision. Forest Press agreed to fund a research project to be administered by the Library Association, and the proposal for the revision submitted by my Department was accepted. A research assistant was appointed in September 1974, and work on the revision was conducted over the next ten months. During that time the LADDCC established a Working Party on Music, comprising eminent music librarians, whose terms of reference were to comment on the work of the revision as it proceeded. This Working Party met on four occasions and provided a valuable forum for the discussion of ideas emanating from the research team. A report to Forest Press and the Decimal Classification Editorial Policy Committee was presented in 1975, and a paper outlining the proposal published the following year.[2]

The Revision Process

After examination of the arrangemment of music in the major general and special classification schemes, it became clear that the most appropriate model to use was the *British Catalogue of Music Classification*, prepared by E. J. Coates.[3] It was largely Coates' analysis that was used as the basis for the construction of the revised 780's.

The main problems that needed to be addressed were:

1. The need to distinguish between music and music literature;
2. The need for different citation orders for music and music literature;
3. The need to increase the capacity for synthesis;

4. The constraints imposed by the notation of the *DDC*;
5. The recognition of a composer facet, and the need for notation for individual composers;
6. The treatment of music in non-European traditions; and,
7. The constraints imposed by the need to ensure that the revision was compatible with the classification as a whole.

The distinction between music scores and music literature, and the need for different citation orders for the two categories, were factors that were not considered in the editions of *DDC* up to edition 20, and it was primarily because of this that many librarians had rejected the scheme for the arrangement of this class, despite the fact that *DDC* might have been used in other parts of their libraries. Any revision would have to ensure, above all, that these defects were repaired. the distinction between music scores, music recordings and music literature is relatively easy to achieve, since the physical differences between each demand that they be shelved separately. So, the simple device of preceding the notation with an M (music scores), or an R (recordings), would enable the distinction to be made, and this was the device adopted. This then made it possible to use the whole base of the notation 780-789 for all three categories simultaneously.

The analysis of the subject field revealed seven basic characteristics or facets:

Theory	(e. g. Psychology of music)
Elements	(e. g. Tonal systems)
Techniques	(e. g. Aural techniques)
Character	(e. g. Programme music)
Forms	(e. g. Sonata form)
Executant	(e. g. Orchestra)
Composer	(e. g. Beethoven).

However, the citation order requirements for each of the two main categories, music scores and music literature, were held to be different, but both had to be met from the same schedule. The respective citation orders were:

Music Scores:	Executant–Forms–Character
Music Literature:	Composer–Executant–Forms– Character–Techniques–Elements– Theory

Provided that the composer facet was introduced by the last digit of the available notational base, so that a general to special filing order was maintained, it was possible to design the schedules so that both categories could be accommodated.

The outline of the schedules, as they appeared in 1980,[4] was as follows:

780 MUSIC

780.1-9	Standard Subdivisions
781	General principles
781.1	Basic principles
781.2	Elements
781.3-.4	Techniques
781.5-.6	Character and Traditions
781.7-.9	Forms
782-788	Executants
782-783	Voices and vocal music
782	Opera and choral
783	Single voices
784-788	Instruments and their music
784	Orchestras and bands
785	Chamber ensembles
786-788	Specific instruments and their music
786	Keyboard, mechanical, electrophonic, percussion
787	Stringed

788	Wind
789	Composers

It is possible to use this schedule for the classification of material in both categories, music scores and music literature:

Music Scores: Precede each class mark with the prefix M
                 789 Composers would not be used
                 Facets in 781.1-781.4 would not be used.

Music Literature: Classing materials about a composer
                   would necessitate the use of 789.

Having decided on the basic schedule outline and the citation orders to be used, we then had to turn our attention to the notation. One of the greatest constraints in using *DDC* is the limited provision for synthesis, i.e. the ability to combine different parts of the schedules to provide for a compound. It is true that synthesis is possible using *DDC*, but only under certain conditions. What is more, there is only one digit, the 0 (zero) which is provided specifically in the Classification for that purpose. In order to provide for all the possible compounds in the subject field (both music scores and music literature), we had to find some means of overcoming this weakness. We decided to reserve the digit 1 (one) to provide for some of the synthesis required, in addition to the usual 0. This meant that the digit 1 could not be used for any division of a class, as this would create a situation with one class number carrying two different meanings. In the event, there are one or two departures from this rule (e.g. 782.1 Opera), but such occurrences are rare and as a general rule the digit 1 is not used to represent a division in any class. The use of two digits as facet indicators gives the schedules great hospitality to compounds existing in the literature, enabling the classer to provide specific class numbers for those compounds. Using the citation orders given earlier in this paper, it is possible to combine any composer (789), with any executant (782-788), with any form (781.7-.9), with any character (781.5-.6), with any technique (781.3-.4), with any element (781.2), with any theory (781.1), or any combination of the foregoing. Little, if any, of this is possible using the editions of *DDC* up to edition 19.

Editions of *DDC* up to edition 19 did not make systematic provision for music and music literature in traditions other than Wetern (European) art music, so we had to ensure that the schedules would be hospitable to these other cultures and traditions, and as far as possible make the schedules as free as possible from emphasis on one tradition. For example, the schedules of instruments and their music (784-788) are based on the acoustical divisions of the Sachs-Hornbostel Classification.[5] It is believed that the resulting schedules make better provision for other traditions of music (folk, popular, jazz, etc.) than those in the existing schedules of *DDC* up to edition 19.

Finding a notation for individual composers proved to be the most intractable of all the problems. Representing an individual composer by alphabetical symbols would have been the easiest solution, e.g. BEE Beethoven, but such notation was incompatible with the notation of *DDC*. Representation using an alpha-numeric code was also possible, but applying Cutter-Sanborn Tables had to be ruled out because of the clash between those composer codes ending in the digit 1 and the same digit used as a facet indicator. Representation using a numerical code was also possible, but once again there was the problem of the digit 1. *The Proposed Revision ... (PR)* included a list of composers with all three methods as options. There was considerable misunderstanding over this list, due in part to the lack of explanation in that publication. Some commentators saw the absence from the list of a well-known composer with a large musical output as some kind of slight on the composer's stature. The composer facet was only to be used with music literature, and the presence of any composer in the list was based on the existence of at least five monographs on that composer in the Library of Congress Shelf List. This criterion merely followed the editorial rules for the provision of any new class number in *DDC*, with some considerable relaxation I might add.

Between the presentation of the original report to Forest Press in 1975 and the publication of the *PR* in 1980, the schedules were amended in the light of comments made by those who were aware of their existence. The publication of the *PR* made the proposals available to a wider audience, and there followed a series of reviews.[6-10] Most of the reviewers were encouraging, and many made constructive comments leading to modifications to the schedules, which have now been incorporated into edition 20. The general acceptance of the *PR* schedules was also assisted by the fact that several libraries were already applying them by 1987, e.g. Trinity College, Dublin, Trinity and All Saints College, Horsforth, England, Sydney Opera House Library, Latrobe University, Australia, City University, London.[11] *The British Catalogue of Music* began to use the schedules in 1982,[12] thus giving an awareness of their existence to music librarians in the United Kingdom and to all those abroad who subscribed to that publication. A considerable body of evidence of use, and comment, had therefore been utilised in the preparation of the final drafts of class 780 in edition 20 when they were completed in 1988.

The Revised Edition

The 780 schedules in edition 20 reveal some important changes from those of the *PR*, but the fundamental principles upon which the schedules were constructed remain intact, and in many cases the published schedules are the same as those in the *PR*:

780 MUSIC

780.1-9	Standard Subdivisions
781	General principles and musical forms
781.1	Basic principles

781.2	Elements
781.3-.4	Techniques
781.5-.6	Kinds and Traditions of music
781.7	Sacred music
781.8	Forms
782-783	Vocal music
782.1-.9	Opera and choral
783	Single voices
784-788	Instruments and their music
784	Orchestras and bands
785	Ensembles with only one instrument per part
786-788	Specific instruments and their music
786	Keyboard, mechanical, electrophonic, percussion
787	Stringed
788	Wind
789	[Composers option]
789.2-.9	[Traditions of music option]

The most important changes are:

1.   The composer facet at 789 is now provided only as an option. There is still a difference of opinion in the profession about the validity, and primary importance, of the composer in music literature. Many remain convinced that works about a given composer are best grouped together, so although this is not the "authorised" arrangement, it will be possible for those who subscribe to that view to arrange their literature that way.

2.   Forms of music, specifically associated with particular instruments, including the voice, have been removed from 781.7-.9 and incorporated at the appropriate points

in the schedules, e.g. instrumental forms in 784, vocal forms in 782.

3.   There is one major departure from the standard citation order for music literature. Normally the citation order would be: Executant (Performing 'instruments')–Form–Character–etc., but in response to many comments this has been changed in 782-783 Vocal music to: Form–Executant (Performing 'instruments')–Character–etc. This will allow the more helpful grouping of the literature of vocal forms.

4.   There is a major revision of 781.5-.7 Kinds and Traditions of music.

5.   Although the *PR* enabled almost unlimited synthesis, it had recommended that no class number should consist of more than three characteristics, so that very long class numbers were avoided. This limitation has now been removed, allowing individuals to make up their own mind as to how much would be required for a particular collection.

Conclusions

The "Phoenix"[13] revision of 780 Music has been unique in that it is the only revision in *DDC* first published as a proposal, thus giving the profession the opportunity to react before the revision became part of the classification. In addition to the published reviews, a number of professional groups in several countries offered comments on the *PR*, and those libraries that adopted the schedules have provided practical evidence of application of the schedules. As indicated earlier, *The British Catalogue of Music* adopted the *PR* in 1982, so the scheme has been applied to a large body of music scores and music literature. The editors of *DDC* have been grateful for the comments from such a wide cross-section of the profession, and all have been considered in the genesis of the schedules of edition 20. Not everyone will agree with everything in the resulting schedules, but at least it can be said that the practical professional input to the revision of 780 Music has been greater than the input to any other revision of a class in *DDC*.

Notes

1. Lionel Roy McColvin, *Music Libraries*. Original ed. by Lionel Roy McColvin and Harold Reeves; completely rewritten, rev. and extended by Jack Dove (London: Deutsch, 1965).

2. Russell Sweeney, "Music in the Dewey Decimal Classification," *Catalogue & Index* no. 42 (Autumn 1976): 4-6.

3. E. J. Coates, comp., *British Catalogue of Music Classification* (London: British National Biography, 1960).

4. Erich M. von Hornbostel and Curt Sachs, "Classification of Musical Instruments," trans. Anthony Baines and Klaus P. Wachsmann, *Galpin Society Journal* 14 (1961): 3-29.

5. *Proposed Revision of 780 Music: Based on Dewey Decimal Classification and Relative Index*, prepared under the direction of Russell Sweeney and John Clews (Albany, N.Y.: Forest Press, 1980).

6. Geraint J. Philp, "The Proposed Revision of 780 Music and Problems in the Development of Faceted Classification for Music," *Brio* 19 (Spring/Summer 1982): 1-13.

7. Russell Sweeney, "The Proposed Revision of 780 Music ...: A reply [to Geraint Philp]," *Brio* 19 (Autumn/Winter 1982): 47-49.

8. Robert H. Hassell, "Revising the Dewey Music Schedules: Tradition vs. Innovation," *Library Resources & Technical Services* 26 (April 1982): 192-203.

9. Russell Sweeney, "[Response to R. H. Hassell]" *Library Resources & Technical Services* 27 (Jan. 1983): 105-107.

10. Richard B. Wursten, "Review of *Proposed Revision of 780 Music*," *Cataloging & Classification Quarterly* 5, no. 2 (Winter 1984): 57-66.

11. Paul Bentley, "The Dewey Decimal Classification and Music," *Cataloguing Australia* (July-Sept. 1980): 27-42.

12. *British Catalogue of Music* 1st interim issue (London: British Library, Bibliographic Services Division, 1982-   ).

13. A "phoenix" revision is a complete revision of a particular schedule, without reference to the arrangements in previous editions of *DDC*.

Appreciation of 780 Music,
or, Left-Handed Bell Ringing

by

Winton E. Matthews, Jr.

ABSTRACT: This paper describes the new 780 Music schedule, giving an overall view of each of the four major sections (Generalities, Vocal music, Instrumental music, and Optional provision for treatises on composers and traditions of music). The provision of precise numbers of such topics as microtonality, anthems, and melodeons is indicated. The greater degree of synthesis is discussed. This synthesis allows for precise numbers for such topics as harmony in piano sonatas, left-hand techniques in playing the piano, and appreciation of twelve-tone song cycles. In addition, use of the Index and the Manual is mentioned.

General Introduction

As a final result of the deliberations discussed in Russell Sweeney's paper (elsewhere in this volume), a new and radically different 780 Music schedule is a part of Edition 20 of the *Dewey Decimal Classification (DDC)*.[1] We should not forget, though, what has always been true, that the rules used in applying the Classification as a whole also apply to music. For example, following the general rule of application, which states that the application of one subject to another is classed with the subject affected, music therapy classes in medicine, not music. A completely rewritten introduction to the *DDC* explains this and other general rules and the new features of the Classification. One of these new features is the two-level summary that introduces schedules of over forty pages. Using the two-level summary of 780, one can grasp at a glance the dimensions of this new and improved schedule.

Winton E. Matthews, Jr. is Assistant Editor, Dewey Decimal Classification, Decimal Classification Division, Library of Congress, Washington, D. C.

Overview of the Schedule

780 is divided into three major parts -- Generalities 780-781, Vocal music 782-783, and Instrumental music 784-788 -- plus an optional provision for composer and traditions of music 789. Within each of the parts, the normal arrangement of topics is from general to specific.

Generalities 780-781 provides a location for comprehensive works on those topics that are common to both vocal and instrumental music. When the topic is discussed as a part of either vocal or instrumental music, it is classed with the kind of music in 782 to 788. In the span 780.1 to 780.9 are located the standard subdivisions of music, such as general music periodicals (780.5) and the history of music (780.9). The major schools and styles, such as impressionism and neoclassicism, are mentioned in various notes in 780.9. The 780.26 development provides numbers for treatises on music scores, recordings, and texts. However, this is not used for the scores, recordings, and texts themselves, since it was thought that the publication format causes a natural shelving segregation of the scores, the treatises, and the recordings. For libraries wishing to indicate the scores and recordings, options are given at 780 and 780.26.

General topics of music and musical forms are located in 781. Music theory itself is classed at 781; music appreciation and psychological aspects of music in 781.1; elements of music, such as time, pitch, microtonality, and counterpoint, in 781.2; composition, including arrangement, in 781.3; the other techniques of music, such as conducting and recording, in 781.4; and kinds of music like springtime music, ballet music, music for weddings, and protest music in 781.4.

The traditions of music, such as folk, popular, and classical, are given in 781.6. These traditions as a part of either vocal or instrumental music are classed with vocal and instrumental music in 782 to 788. However, if the library limits 781-788 to only one tradition, such as classical music or jazz, the other traditions are classed in 789. None of the options mentioned in this paper will be followed by the Decimal Classification Division of the Library of Congress.

Because the *DDC* is largely based on literary warrant of material located in Western libraries, Christian sacred music is allotted two of the subsections of sacred music, 781.71 and 781.72. 781.71 is used for music by specific denominations, and 781.72 is used for music by specific times of the church year. As *DDC* is also an international classification, the sacred music of other religions is provided for in 781.73-781.79 (e.g., 781.745 for Hindu sacred music).

Musical forms that are not limited to either vocal or instrumental music are classed in 781.8. Included here are da capo, rondo, and ground-bass forms. Vocal forms are classed in 782.1 to 782.4, instrumental forms in 784.18.

The second major part of the schedule is vocal music, which covers 782 and 783. The basic arrangement for this part is vocal forms in 782.1-782.4, multiple voices in combination in 782.5-782.9, single voices in combination in 783.1, and solo voices in 783.2-783.9. Voices are subarranged by sex and then by range. General studies of the voice itself are classed in 783. Vocal forms are subarranged into dramatic vocal forms, such as opera and musical plays, in 782.1; sacred vocal forms (other than services), such as anthems and hymns, in 782.2; music for religious services in 782.3; and secular forms, such as madrigals and song cycles, in 782.4. Staging dramatic music is classed in 792.5, a subdivision of theater.

The subarrangement of 784-788 for instrumental music, which follows the same pattern as that for vocal music, is from general topics through instruments in combination to individual instruments. In 784.1 are found general topics of instrumental music, instrumental forms, and general works about instruments. Instrumental forms, such as sonata, symphony, concerto, and nocturne, have their own number. The development for works about instruments contains construction, tuning, geographical treatment and techniques for playing, such as breathing and fingering. Assembly-line construction of instruments is classed in 681.8.

Instrumental ensembles with more than one instrument per part, i.e., the various orchestral combinations and bands, are found in 784.2-784.9, e.g., symphony orchestras at 784.2. Those with only one instrument per part are classed in 785, the number used for chamber music. 785 is subarranged by instrument, thus providing precise numbers for ensembles, such as wind ensembles and guitar quartets.

Specific instruments and their music are found in 786-788. The subarrangement of these parts is based on the Sachs-Hornbostel arrangement.[2] The Music Library Association's "Proposed Revision of MARC Field 048" was also consulted during work on the final version of 780.[3] Therefore, even though the majority of instruments given in the schedules are traditional Western instruments, nontraditional Western and other instruments have a place, if not a precise number, in the schedule. If five or more books about an instrument were found in the Library of Congress collection, the instrument is mentioned in both the schedule and in the Index. For example, biwas, citterns, and shamisens are given in a note under the heading Flat-back lute family at 787.85. If one to four books were found, the instruments, such as gaitas, hichirikis, and santirs, are given only in the Index.

The instruments section is divided into stringed instruments (chordophones) at 787, wind instruments (aerophones) at 788, and all other instruments at 786. Keyboard instruments are found in 786.2 to 786.5, mechanical instruments in 786.6, electrophonic instruments and electronic music in 786.7. 786.8 is used for percussion instruments in general and specific instruments other than drums, the latter being classed in 786.9. Precise numbers are given in 786.8 for celestas and hand bells. Stringed instruments provided in 787 include violins, zithers, guitars, and many others. A few of the wind instruments given in 788 are flutes, recorders, bagpipes, saxophones, and melodeons.

As previously mentioned, 789 is an optional number. One of its uses is to provide a location for other traditions of music when 781 to 788 is reserved for a single tradition. The other use is to allow for arrangement of treatises first by composer. The standard arrangement of treatises is not by composer but by the type of work. For example, works about Beethoven are classed with composers of all types of music in 780.92, while *Fidelio* is classed with opera in 782.1, the piano concertos with orchestral music in 784.262186, and the piano sonatas with the piano as solo instrument in 786.2183. However, a library may wish to have all treatises about Beethoven and his works together in one array. This can be done by using 789 plus an alphabeting mark plus the notation following 78 in 780 to 788. For example, works about Beethoven 789.Be, *Fidelio* 789.Be21, piano concertos 789.Be4262186, piano sonatas 789.Be62183.

Ordering the Facets

The numbers just used are examples of how this schedule sets down the various facets that have been discussed. The first question when dealing with multiple facets is "What is the order of precedence for the facets?" The other question is "Can each of the facets be indicated, and if so, how?" The rest of the paper will answer these questions, but with the proviso that not all of the exceptions given in the schedule will be discussed.

The first rule is that a topic coming later in the schedule takes precedence over earlier topics. For example, harmony in piano sonatas has three facets: the general principle, harmony; the instrument, piano; the musical form, sonata. General works on harmony class in 781.25, on the piano in 786.2, and on the sonata form in 784.183. Using the rule that later topics take precedence over earlier ones, one derives the correct order of precedence: piano, sonata form, harmony.

The second rule is to prefer the executant of the music, be it instrument or voice either alone or in combination, over the form of music. For example, Beethoven's *Symphony No. 9 in D minor* is a work in the symphony form for orchestra with vocal parts. The executant, orchestra with vocal parts, is preferred over the form, symphony. This example also follows the first rule since orchestra with vocal parts is classed in 784.22 and symphony form is classed in 784.184.

The major exceptions to the rule of executant over form occur with vocal music. Treatises, recordings, texts, and scores of dramatic vocal forms all class with the form in 782.1, not with the voices that are singing in 782.5-783.9. It was thought that the vocal form was more important than the voices producing the music. Moreover, how many people know exactly what the vocal requirements are for Verdi's *Aida* and Holst's *Savitri*? *Aida* requires a soprano, a mezzo-soprano, two tenors, a baritone, two basses, and chorus, plus 98 non-singing spear carriers; while *Savitri* requires a soprano, a tenor, and a baritone. With nondramatic vocal music, a patron interested in reading about or listening to a singer or a piece of music will usually not know the singer's vocal range or the vocal requirements of that piece of music. In contrast, a patron interested in scores for nondramatic music will know the type of voice or voices involved, e.g., a song cycle sung by a soprano, or a mass sung by a tenor and male chorus. Therefore, treatises about and recordings of singers and nondramatic vocal forms are classed with the form in 782.2 to 782.4, while the scores and texts are classed in 782.5-783.9. With instrumental music, most people interested in reading about or listening to a piece know what instruments are required because the instruments are normally a part of the title or subtitle of the work. Therefore, the music, treatises, and recordings of a specific type of instrumental music all class in the same number. The same principle also applies to the instrumentalists.

Another important rule that applies not only to 780 Music but also to the rest of the *DDC* is to read and follow the notes not only at the number but also at the superior numbers. For example, where does music for Baptist weddings class? Music for weddings is classed in 781.587, and Baptist sacred music in 781.7161 (see Figure 1). It would seem that the rule of classing with the later number would mean that music for Baptist weddings would class in 781.7161. Alas, this is not true; for at 781.7, a number superior to 781.7161, there is a note instructing that sacred music accompanying stages of the life cycle (of which weddings is one) is classed in 781.58. Thus, music for Baptist weddings is classed in 781.587, not 781.7161.

Figure 1

Music for Baptist Weddings 781.587

781.58	*Music accompanying stages of the life cycle

. . .

781.587	*Weddings and marriage

. . .

781.7	**Sacred Music**

Class sacred music accompanying stages of life cycle in 781.58

. . .

781.711-.718	Of specific denominations

Add to base number 781.71 the numbers following -2 in notation 21-28 from Table 7, e.g., Baptist sacred music 781.7161

One of the new kinds of notes in edition 20 is the *See Manual* note. In 1982 the *Manual on the Use of the Dewey Decimal Classification: Edition 19* was published as a separate.[4] The *Manual* discussed problems of choice of discipline and of precedence and citation order and reflected on the practices of the Decimal Classification Division at the Library of Congress. For edition 20, the *Manual* is an integral part of the edition and is referred to by *See Manual* notes. Since 780 is a completely new schedule, the *Manual*

contains an eleven-page introduction to 780, which covers much of
the same ground as this paper. In addition, specific problems are
covered in detail. For instance, how should one class a book that
seems to criticize both the opera itself and its staging? 782.1 is the
number for the music of operas, 792.5 the number for staging operas
(see Figure 2). Which one should be used in this instance? At both
782.1 and 792.5 there is the note *See Manual at 792.5 vs. 782.1*. In
the *Manual* section of edition 20 at 792.5 vs. 782.1 there is a
discussion of what is to be classed in each number. Also, there is the
statement that if one is in doubt between the two numbers, 782.1 is
preferred. From this statement one can infer that 782.1 is the correct
number for the book being classed.

Figure 2

Music of Opera vs. Staging Operas, 782.1 vs. 792.5

782.1   ***Dramatic vocal forms   *Operas**

. . .

See Manual at 792.5 vs. 782.1

. . .

792.5   **†Opera**

. . .

See Manual at 792.5 vs. 782.1

. . .

792.5 vs.   **[Staging] Opera vs. [Musical aspects of]**
782.1   **Dramatic vocal forms**

Class in 782.1 works that discuss dramatic vocal
forms as a type of vocal music, including such
topics as tempos, plots, singers, conducting.
Class in 792.5 works that discuss dramatic vocal
forms as a type of stage presentation, including
such topics as costumes, sets, direction. Works

about an opera house and its productions are
classed in 792.509, e.g., a history of La Scala,
Milan 782.5094521. If in doubt, class in 782.1.

Indicating the Facets

Now that the facets have been ordered correctly, the next step
is to determine whether or not they can be indicated. If the facet is
given in a "class-here" note or is the same or approximately the same
as a number's heading, other facets can be indicated. If the facet is
given in either an example or an "including" note, other facets
cannot be indicated. For example, as previously mentioned, the
correct order of precedence for harmony in piano sonatas is piano,
sonata form, harmony. Since these topics are the headings at 786.2,
784.183, and 781.25, respectively, further facets can be indicated.
For harmony in a mazurka for piano, the precedence order is piano,
mazurka, harmony. Because the mazurka is a part of the "example"
note at 784.1884, further facets, such as harmony, cannot be
indicated.

Once it has been determined whether or not further facets can
be indicated, synthesis of the notation for each facet occurs through
the use of "add" notes and tables. Standard subdivision facets are
added to music through the use of a table. For example, in the table
of standard subdivisions, 05 is the notation for periodicals. When the
notation is added to 781.25 Harmony, the number 781.2505 means
periodicals about harmony. In like manner, 786.205 means
periodicals about piano music. Please note that the zero is used as a
facet indicator, a feature familiar to users of previous editions of the
DDC.

In developing this schedule, it was decided that to show the
various facets available within 780 a method of synthesis similar to
the use of 0 (zero) needed to be introduced. As Russell Sweeney noted

in his paper, this was done by using both zero and the digit 1 (one), wherever possible, as facet indicators. In a few instances, the 1 has a special meaning, such as in 782.1 for Dramatic vocal music. But, in most instances, the facet indicator 1 is used to introduce a general topic of music or a musical form. Instructions on the use of 0 and 1 are given in various add tables and notes throughout 780. For example, the notation for harmony in piano sonatas is synthesized as follows. At 786.2 Pianos (the first facet) there is a note to add as instructed in the add table under the centered entry at 784-788 (see Figure 3). The instruction in the add table says that musical forms and instruments are shown by adding 1, then the numbers following 784.1 in 784.18-784.19. Thus, facet indicator 1 plus 83 from 784.183 Sonata form added to 786.2 produces 786.2183 Piano sonatas. At 784.183 is the instruction to add as instructed under the centered entry at 781.2-781.8, which says to show general principles add 1 and then the numbers following 781 in 781.1-781.7. The result of adding 1 to 25 from 781.25 Harmony is 786.2183125 harmony in piano sonatas.

Figure 3

Harmony in Piano Sonatas 786.2183125

781.25   ***Harmony**
. . .
*Add as instructed under 781.2-781.8
. . .
784.183   †Sonata forms
. . .
*Add as instructed under 781.2-781.8

786.2   ***Pianos**
. . .
*Add as instructed under 784-788
. . .

781.2-781.8 Other principles and musical forms

Add to notation for each term identified by * as follows:
   01-09 Standard subdivisions
         Notation from Table 1 as modified at 780.1-780.9,
         e.g., performances 078

   1   General principles
         Add to 1 the numbers following 781 in 781.1-781.7, e.g.,
         rock music 166, rehearsing rock music 166144

                    . . .

784-788 Instruments and their music

Add to notation for each term identified by * as follows:
   01-09 Standard subdivisions
          Notation from Table 1 as modified at 780.1-
          780.9, e.g., performances 078
            See Manual at 784-788: Add table: 092

   1   General principles, musical forms, instruments
   11-17 General principles
          Add to 1 the numbers following 781 in 781.1-
          781.7, e.g., performance techniques 143
            *For techniques for playing instruments, see
            193*

   18-19 Musical forms and instruments
          Add to 1 the numbers following 784.1 in
          784.18-784.19, e.g., sonata form 183,
          techniques for playing instruments 193

In like manner, various facets can be combined. For example,
a book on left-hand techniques in playing the piano is classed in
786.1219366, which is developed from 786.2 Piano and 784.19366
Left-hand techniques in playing an instrument.

Left-hand techniques in playing
   the piano   786.219366
      Piano   786.2
      Facet indicator   1
      Left-hand techniques   9366 (from 784.19366)

In like manner, 786.88485 Hand bells synthesized with 784.19366 produces 786.8848519366, the number for left-handed hand-bell ringing.

Left-handed hand-bell ring	786.8848519366
Hand bells	786.88485
Facet indicator	1
Left-hand techniques	9366 (from 784.19366)

The number for the appreciation of twelve-tone song cycles is 782.471268117. This number can be broken into its facets: 782.4, song cycles, 268 from 781.268 twelve-tone system, and 17 from 781.17 appreciation.

Appreciation of twelve-tone song cycles	782.471268117
Song cycles	782.47
Facet indicator	1
Twelve-tone system	268 (from 781.268)
Facet indicator	1
Appreciation	17 (from 781.17)

This synthesis can be used to analyze parts of larger works, if no limit is placed on the amount of synthesis. For example, a work on the recording of trumpet music is classed in 788.92149, from 788.92 Trumpets and 781.49 Recording of music.

Recording trumpet music	788.92149
Trumpets	788.92
Facet indicator	1
Recording of music	49 (from 781.49)

A subsection of this work could be on recording military fanfares for trumpets, for which the number is 788.92189241599149.

Recording of fanfares for trumpets	788.9218924149
Trumpets	788.92
Facet indicator	1

Fanfares	8924 (from 784.18924)
Facet indicator	1
Recording of music	49 (from 781.49)

Or even more narrowly, 788.921892415991534149 for indoor military fanfares for trumpets.

Recording of military fanfares for trumpets	788.92189241599149
Trumpets	788.92
Facet indicator	1
Fanfares	8924 (from 784.18924)
Facet indicator	1
Military music	599 (from 781.599)
Facet indicator	1
Recording of music	49 (from 781.49)

As one can easily see, this ability to synthesize facets is a powerful tool, but it can become unwieldy. Therefore, it was decided that the ability to indicate facets should be limited to adding 0 or 1 just two times (with an option to add as many times as desired). Even this limit might still produce numbers too long for a library. One can always shorten a *DDC* number by eliminating one or more digits after the decimal point. This elimination can at times produce numbers that are not useful. In the 780s an excellent method to shorten a number is to eliminate the 0 or 1 and all following digits after the decimal point.

As I hope I have made clear, the new 780 in edition 20 is a schedule with provisions that are arranged in a clear and logical sequence and with a greater ability to synthesize numbers than ever before.

Notes

1.   Melvil Dewey, *Dewey Decimal Classification and Relative Index*, 20th ed., ed. John P. Comaromi, et al. (Albany, N.Y.: Forest Press, 1989).

2.   Erich M. von Hornbostel and Curt Sachs, "Classification of Musical Instruments," trans. Anthony Baines and Klaus P. Wachsmann, *Galpin Society Journal* 14 (1961): 3-29.

3.   Working Group on Access via Medium of Performance, Music Library Association, "Proposed Revision of MARC Field 048" (Preliminary draft, February 1983 [revised: January 1984]) (Photocopy).

4.   *Manual on the Use of the Dewey Decimal Classification: Edition 19*, prepared by John P. Comaromi and Margaret J. Warren (Albany, N.Y.: Forest Press, 1982).

Online Music Subject Retrieval
Using the New Schedule
by
Arnold S. Wajenberg

ABSTRACT: Subject searches are more frequent in online catalogs, but
often unsuccessful. Classifications can be used to add another dimension to
subject retrieval. *DDC* lends itself to online subject retrieval because of the
simplicity of its notation, its hierarchical arrangement, and its synthesis of
notation. A proposed system for MARC content designation of *DDC* music
class numbers is described, and a potential user interface is discussed.

Research into the use of online catalogs has demonstrated that
those using these catalogs perform subject searches far more
frequently than do users of card catalogs. The same investigations
have shown that these subject searches are often unsuccessful. The
result has been an increasing attention to ways of improving subject
retrieval in online catalogs. Often these efforts focus on
supplementing controlled subject vocabularies such as the *Library of
Congress Subject Headings* with key word access to data such as
titles and tables of contents. However, there has also been an
interest in using classification as a supplement to subject retrieval
using topical headings.

Classification has the capability of adding another dimension
to subject retrieval. A subject heading assembles related material
under a single heading. A classification scheme assembles related
subjects or topics into an ordered system. This allows a significant
enrichment of subject retrieval. Library patrons utilize this
capability now when they browse a collection that is arranged in
classified order. Some online systems now permit a similar browsing
through an online version of a library's shelflist. However, it is

Arnold S. Wajenberg is Principal Cataloger, University of Illinois Library at
Urbana-Champaign.

possible to make much more sophisticated use of classification in online systems.

The *Dewey Decimal Classification (DDC)* lends itself to online subject retrieval because of the simplicity of its notation, and especially because hierarchical relationships are usually expressed by the length of the numbers. For example:

786	Keyboard, mechanical, electrophonic, percussion instruments.
786.5	Keyboard wind instruments. Organs.
786.55	Reed organs and regals.

If someone wanted information about reed organs, it could be sought under either the appropriate subject heading or under the class number 786.55. If insufficient information was found on the specific subject, the search under classification could easily be broadened by dropping the last digit, and searching 786.5 for books on organs. These might well include information on reed organs. Similarly, the search could be broadened still more by searching 786 for books on keyboard instruments in general.

Sometimes, in order to avoid unduly long numbers, the editors of *DDC* use numbers of the same length for a topic and its subtopics. An example of this is the number for left-hand techniques referred to in Matthews' paper (elsewhere in this volume). It fits into this hierarchy:

784.193	Techniques for playing instruments.
784.1936	Arm techniques
784.19365	Hand techniques.
784.19366	Left-hand techniques.

The number for left-hand techniques and the number for hand techniques are both 8 digits long; hierarchy is not expressed in the length of numbers. In this situation, a computer could not automatically broaden a search by shortening the class number.

Another feature of *DDC* that has great potential for online subject retrieval is its provision for built or synthesized numbers, which are described in the papers by Sweeney and Matthews (elsewhere in this volume). However, for this potential to be realized, the elements of a synthesized class number must be identifiable to a computer program. In September of 1983, I published an article "MARC Coding of DDC for Subject Retrival," in which solutions are proposed for the problems just mentioned.[1] The solutions require defining values for the second indicator position after 082 and 092, the MARC tags for *DDC* numbers. Additional subfields are also recommended for these two tags.

Although it now seems likely that these problems will be solved in part by the provisions of an authority record for class numbers, which is now being developed at the Library of Congress, the solutions proposed in the 1983 article still seem valid. The remainder of this paper describes how the system discussed in the 1983 article would be applied to the numbers in the new *DDC* schedule for music.

In order to solve the problem of making hierarchy identifiable to a computer program when length of number does not express hierarchy, two indicator values are recommmended in the second indicator position. Indicator value 2 would be used to mean that the closest superordinate element in the hierarchy is classed in the immediately preceding number of the same length. Indicator value 3 would be used to mean that the closest superordinate element in the hierarchy is classed in a number of the same length that is not the immediately preceding class number. Subfield d was recommended for storing the class number for the immediately superordinate element in the hierarchy. Under this system, the example given above would be coded as follows:

082 02   784.19366 $2 20
          (Left-hand techniques)
082 03   784.19367 $d 784.19365 $2 20
          (Right-hand techniques)

Indicator value 2 shows that the preceding number, 784.19365, is the class number for hand techniques, the next most general concept in the hierarchy. Indicator value 3 before 784.19367, the number for right-hand techinques, shows that the class number for hand techniques is recorded in subfield d. The following kind of search would be possible in an online catalog programmed to utilize this system of coding. Someone seeking information on left-hand techniques could be led to the appropriate class number, 784.19366. If insufficient information was found there, the indicator value 2 would permit the system to identify 784.19365 as the class number for hand techniques, the nearest superordinate element in the hierarchy. Similarly, if someone seeking information about right-hand techniques found insufficient information in 784.19367, the system could identify 784.19365 as the next most general number.

In order to permit a program to recognize and manipulate synthesized class numbers, several additional subfields are recommended:

      a   Complete, synthesized class number.
      e   Base number, from classification schedule
      f   Table number
      g   Number from table
      h   Source class number.

The previous example, of someone seeking information on left-hand techniques, can be used to demonstrate how this system would function. It is assumed that the searcher wanted an exhaustive list of the library's materials on this subject, and that the library had a few books on left-hand techniques generally, but also had works on left-hand techniques in playing the piano, the harpsichord, the organ, the reed organ, the kettledrum, and hand bells. As Matthews has shown, *DDC* 20 permits the general number for left-hand techniques , 784.19366, to serve as a source number in building synthesized numbers for works on left-hand techniques in playing specific instruments. Under the system here recommended, the class

numbers for the various works on the subject held by the
hypothetical library would be coded as follows:

```
082  02  784.19366 $2 20
                (Left-hand techniques)
082  02  786.219366 $e 786.2 $h 784.19366 $2 20
                (786.2 = Piano)
082  02  786.419366 $e 786.4 $h 784.19366 $2 20
                (786.4 = Harpsichord)
082  02  786.519366 $e 786.5 $h 784.19366 $2 20
                (786.5 = Organ)
082  02  786.5519366 $e 786.55 $h 784.19366  $2 20
                (786.55 = Reed organ)
082  02  786.8848519366 $e 786.88485 $h 784.19366 $2 20
                (786.88485 = Hand bells)
082  02  786.9319366 $e 786.93 $h 784.19366  $2 20
                (786.93 = Kettledrum).
```

An online catalog coded to recognize synthesized class
numbers would make it possible for a user of the catalog to retrieve
not only the works classed in the general number for left-hand
techniques, 784.19366, but also the works classed in every
synthesized class number in which 784.19366 was stored in subfield
h. Furthermore, the use of second indicator value 2 with each of
these class numbers would inform the system that works on the more
general topic, hand techniques, would be classed in the immediately
preceding number of the same length for each of these instruments
(786.219365, 786.419365, 786.519365, 786.5519365, etc.).

Additional subfields are suggested for numbers formed using
the tables in volume 1 of *DDC*. Table 1 contains numbers called
"standard subdivisions," which can be added to any class number,
unless there are specific instructions not to use them. Their use can
best be understood from an example. One set of standard
subdivisions is made up of numbers beginning 08, for treatment of
the subject of the class number with respect to kinds of persons. The

set includes 083 for young people and children. A work on left-hand technique for children playing musical instruments would be classed 784.19366083; a work on left-hand technique for children playing the piano would be classed 786.219366083. In the system recommended here, these numbers would be coded as follows:

```
082  02  784.19366083 $e 784.19366 $f 1 $g 083 $2 20
082  02  786.219366083 $e 786.2 $f 1 $g 083 $h 784.19366
              $2 20
```

It is not uncommon for online catalogs to have such capabilities as right-hand truncation and boolean searching. These capabilities could be employed very effectively with the coding system recommended here. If # is used to represent truncation, and .a. to represent the boolean "and," it would be possible to enter a search for every occurrence of the truncated class number 784.193# in either subfield a or subfield h, combined with .a. 1 in subfield f .a. 083 in subfield g. This would permit an exhaustive search for works on all kinds of techniques for playing all kinds of musical instruments by children.

This is, of course, a very complex system. If it is to work effectively, a great deal of attention must be given to the user interface. It is unrealistic to expect users of libraries to understand either the intricacies of the *DDC* or the complexities of MARC coding. It is also obviously unrealistic to expect them to master a controlled vocabulary such as the *Library of Congress Subject Headings*. They can be expected to enter terms that they identify as expressing the topic in which they are interested. Eventually, online catalogs must be able to match these relatively free-text searches from catalog users with controlled vocabularies and captions from classification schedules.

Probably a dialogue between the searcher and the system will be required. It might proceed along these lines. The searcher might enter: "Subject: how to use the left hand when playing musical instruments." This will certainly not match any subject heading or caption from a classification schedule. The system might apply a stop word list that would eliminate prepositions, articles and conjunctions from consideration, and then search the remaining words, singly and in combination, in indexes of titles and contents notes. Some works might be retrieved in this way, which could be listed for the searcher. Also, subject headings and class numbers used for these books could also be retrieved. The subject headings and captions for the class numbers could be displayed, with a question asking the searcher if (s)he wishes to view titles listed under any of them.

It seems at least possible that the class number for left-hand techniques might be retrieved, either independently or as part of a synthesized class number. That would make possible the kind of retrieval described in this paper.

As Sweeney and Matthews have shown, the new *DDC* 780 schedule is a rigorously faceted scheme, which makes it possible to add any topic in the general numbers, such as 780 and 781, to the more specific numbers that follow. The coding system which is suggested here would make it possible for an online catalog to retrieve material classed in any of the general numbers, and also in all specific numbers synthesized from those general numbers.

Note

1.   Arnold S. Wajenberg, "MARC Coding of *DDC* for Subject Retrieval," *Information Technology and Libraries* 2 (1983): 246-251.

Radical Change with Minimal Disruption:
The Effect of Revised 780 Music
on the University of Illinois
Library Shelf Arrangement[1]

by

Charles Forrest and Richard P. Smiraglia

ABSTRACT: A study to assess the impact of the *Proposed Revision...* *(PR)* of 780 Music on shelf arrangement of books is described. The study was designed to discover: a) the proportion of books that would have different class numbers using the *PR* rather than *DDC* 19; b) the most populous classes and the subject areas growing the fastest; c) the impact of potential dislocation on browsability; d) the effect of expanded synthesis on class numbers; and e) whether online subject retrieval would be enhanced using the *PR*. A random sample of books classed in *DDC* 19 were reclassed using the *PR*. It was found that intershelving would not create major disturbances because most books fell into unique classes that will not conflict, or into hierarchical arrangements that have not changed in the *PR*.

Introduction

A substantial revision of the music (780) schedule in the Dewey Decimal Classification (*DDC*) has been needed for many years. *DDC* provisions for music have remained essentially unchanged throughout its history. Many libraries found the classification ineffective because of its organization of music based on the size of performing ensemble, and they were forced to search for alternatives.[2] Much musical scholarship, particularly the study of ethnic musics, has never been satisfactorialy incorporated into the

---

Charles Forrest is Director of Instructional Support Serivces at the Candler Library, Emory University, and formerly Assistant Undergraduate Librarian and Media Coordinator, Undergraduate Library, University of Illinois at Urbana-Champaign. Richard P. Smiraglia is Senior Lecturer, School of Library Service, Columbia University, formerly Music Catalog Librarian, University of Illinois at Urbana-Champaign.

schedules. This is surprising given *DDC*'s flexibility in the area of geographical and cultural subdivision.

The purpose of the study reported here was to assess the impact of *The Proposed Revision ... (PR)* on shelf arrangement of books about music in the University of Illinois Library, especially those collections on open shelves. The complete revision (or, "phoenix schedule") was prepared under the direction of Russell Sweeney and John Clews.[3] In an historic first for *DDC*, the *PR* was issued as a separate publication in 1980 and response was solicited from the profession.

Literature Review

In a 1982 review, Geraint J. Philp discussed the revised schedule as an example of faceted classification. In a faceted classification, symbols representing mutually exclusive and collectively exhaustive concepts are combined in a prescribed sequence to represent any subject. While *DDC* exhibits many synthetic features, allowing symbols from various parts of the schedules or from special tables to be combined with other numbers, true faceting is unusual in the *DDC* and remains unfamiliar to many librarians in the United States. Philp pointed to many murky relations and clumsy arrangements of numbers within the *PR*. For example:

> Intervals at 781.237 should be closer to melody at 781.24, while consonance at 781.238 and dissonance at 781.239 should be under harmony at 781.25 .... The foci [should be] ordered within the facets along the lines of historical evolution of the subject, such as the development of tonal systems at 781.26 and forms at 781.7-781.9. Thus in 781.26, modes and macrotonality would be better preceding diatonicism, while there is no mention of bi- and polytonality. Also to have 'dodecaphony (twelve-tone system, note rows)" at 781.268 under tonal systems only confuses, because atonality is already at 781.267 and serialism under techniques at 781.33.[4]

Philp went on to discuss the schedule's relationship to printed music, and the field and literature of music. He made only fleeting references to the way materials might be wanted on a hypothetical shelf.

In an article that appeared in 1982, Robert H. Hassell attempted to assess the differences between the proposed schedules and *DDC* 19 "from the standpoint of performers ... seeking chamber music."[5] This he did by classifying a sample of 400 ensemble scores according to each scheme, and then comparing each resulting order "with the order deemed most advantageous for those seeking to retrieve such scores for performance purposes."[6] Hassell's performance-oriented arrangement was based on five principles of which three predominated: 1) all music for a particular performing medium (whether in solo, or as focus for an ensemble work) should be kept together; 2) arrangements and original works should not be intermingled, but arrangements should be kept as a group immediately following original music for the medium of focus; and 3) subfiling within a category should be general-special, thus collections should be arranged alphabetically by title, followed by individual composers arranged alphabetically by composer, with collections again preceding separate works arranged by title and opus number.

Neither *DDC* 19 nor the *PR* performed well in Hassell's test, with the proportion of scores that matched the desired arrangement calculated as 38% for *DDC* 19 and 41% for the *PR*. Tests of statistical significance showed that the observed slight improvement in the performance of the *PR* was not statistically significant (thus it is possible that the observed difference could have been attributed to chance). In either scheme, only a few categories demonstrated better than 50% compliance with Hassell's performance-oriented arrangement although minor improvements in the collocation of media were observed in the *PR*; vocal music and string ensembles among them. The weakest category, in which the scores were dispersed rather than collocated according to his performance criterion, was the section for keyboard music.

Hassell's study indicated that neither *DDC* 19 nor its proposed revision were effective at medium collocation or at general-special subarrangement. Because there was no statistically significant difference between the measured effectiveness of the two schedules on his criteria he concluded that "the decision as to whether to adopt or reject the proposed scheme must be made on some other basis than its utility for the classification of chamber music ...."[7] In his concluding discussion, Hassell pointed out:

> There is also little doubt that classification in a faceted scheme is more complex, time-consuming, and therefore more expensive than in an enumerative scheme, and in this case the data fail to support the hypothesis that the result will be enough *improvement in shelf arrangement to justify the effort and expense.*[8]

In the most comprehensive review of the proposed schedule, which appeared in 1984, Richard B. Wursten discussed the significant innovations, including a greater capacity for number building "allowing the Dewey users for the first time to express extremely complex concepts through the construction of lengthy class numbers with faceted characteristics."[9] The increased length of call numbers, however, could pose problems in shelf-reading and reshelving. As Wursten pointed out, the use of facet indicators necessitated a wholesale restructuring of the schedule. An inspection of the *PR*'s "List of Changed Numbers" suggested that most numbers would be significantly different, confounding browsing. Wursten identified as the least successful feature the two composers' tables at 789, which were intended to furnish either chronological or alphabetical arrangement of biography of major composers. Only 307 composers were represented, which might tempt librarians to "concoct their own numbers for composers not listed to interfile with those that are listed."[10] Despite attempts to integrate Western and non-Western performing media, the only discrete provision for musics other than Western art is an alternative section at 789.9. This section contains subdivisions for such diverse types of music as folk music, popular music, jazz and all non-Western traditions.

Response to the *PR* was nearly universally negative concerning the proposed composers' list at 789. Some respondents preferred arrangement of works about music by form, rather than executant. Response to the use of the digit 1 (one) as a facet indicator was positive, and it was suggested that restrictions on the number of additions be removed. Though the integration of Western and non-Western performing media was lauded for use by libraries collecting in only one tradition, it was considered unwieldy for libraries that collect comprehensively and wish to class exemplars of music from non-Western traditions apart from those of Western art music. It was suggested that biography be returned to 780.9ff. and that 789 be reserved for culture or geographic based-classification of non-Western art musics.[11]

Many of the faults that reviewers found in the *PR* have been corrected for the revised schedule that appeared in *DDC* 20. Restrictions on the number of facets that may be used were made optional. The composers list was removed from 789, and the use of 780.92 for biography remains a valid option. Traditions of music were expanded from 781.62ff. to 781.62-781.69.[12]

The Study

The study was designed to seek answers to the following specific questions:

1.   What proportion of books would have classification numbers from the *PR* that would differ from those assigned using *DDC* 19? Based on an inspection of the "List of Changed Numbers" in the proposed revision it appeared that a majority of titles could potentially be classed in different places.

2.   What were the most populous classes and in which subject areas were the collections growing most rapidly? Regardless of the amount of change in the schedules, dislocation (that is, classification of material on one topic into

two different classification numbers) would be irrelevant in areas where books were not being acquired. Conversely, in areas of music literature that were rapidly expanding (due to research trends and/or collection development priorities) integration of material on different topics in one number would be especially problematic.

 3.   What would be the impact of such dislocation on the browsability of the shelves? In addition to the problems of integration and dislocation addressed above, what would be the effect on the hierarchical sequence of intershelving diverse topical material? Related topics might no longer collocate, thus confounding browsing.

 4.   What effect would the use of the expanded synthetic provisions have on classification numbers created using the *PR*? It seemed likely that numbers would at least be potentially longer and more complex. Depending on the exclusivity and mnemonic features of the facets this could be a boon, or it could further confound browsing.

 5.   Could subject retrieval in the online catalog be appreciably enhanced through use of the *PR*? UIUC library users were already accustomed to the shelf position search capability of the LCS system. Originally designed to facilitate shelflisting, this feature had proven valuable for comprehensive examination of subject holdings regardless of stack location.

ASSUMPTIONS

The following assumptions were made:

 1.   There would be no reclassification of existing material following implementation of the *PR*.

 2.   As a consequence of the first assumption, intershelving of mixed subject material would take place.

3.   All synthetic features would be employed with no limitation on the length of classification numbers.[13]

4.   Retrospective conversion of the UIUC book shelflist took place in 1978;[14] thus subsequent dates of entry into the database corresponded to the date of acquisition of the item.

LIMITATION

Specificity would be observed—that is, in the event a treatise discussed two or three distinct topics, the classification number would reflect the predominant topic, or lacking predominance, the first topic. For works treating more than three topics the classification would reflect a broader topic encompassing the contents.

METHODOLOGY

The University Library at the University of Illinois at Urbana-Champaign (UIUC) is a decentralized campus library system with a central bookstacks and thirty-eight departmental libraries. Library material is classified using *DDC* with the major exception of the Law Library, Asian Library, scores and sound recordings in the Music Library, [15] and the government documents collection. Collection development patterns have concentrated monographs on music (780-789) in the Music Library, the Undergraduate Library, and the central bookstacks. The sixteenth edition of the *DDC* was used until the adoption of *DDC* 19 in December of 1980.

The UIUC Library Computer System (LCS) contains brief circulation records for all cataloged library materials in the campus library system. One way of searching this system is by call number (the shelf position search). At the time of the study, there were approximately 37,000 items in the range of call numbers from 780 to, but not including, 790. To achieve results at a 90% confidence level

± 5% (deemed sufficient for management decision making) a sample size of 270 was required. A sample of 366 records was selected using sequential shelf position searches from a randomly selected starting point. A personal computer interfaced with LCS was used to draw every 100th record beginning with an initial record randomly selected from the first one hundred records. The program utilized a shelf position search command, beginning with the initial record, and continued until the 100th record was reached, which was then downloaded onto a diskette. The program continued until the call number 790 was reached. The downloaded records were printed. These items were retrieved from the shelves.

Items not on the shelf, charged out, missing or lost, reduced the actual sample size to 279 records. The proportional results reported here may be safely generalized to academic research collections of books about music whose collection development patterns parallel those of the UIUC Library.

Surrogates of the items in the sample were constructed by photocopying the title pages and their versos, tables of contents, and additional information (such as prefaces or indexes) that would assist in assigning classification numbers to the pieces. Visible call numbers on the photocopies, including those appearing in CIP information, were obliterated. The sample titles were then classified by the researchers using the *PR*. Because the UIUC libraries classified using the 16th edition of *DDC* until the adoption of *DDC* 19 (December, 1980), the additional step was taken of reclassifying material cataloged before December 1980 into *DDC* 19 (229 items). The entire sample was then reviewed for consistency in application of the schedules.

RESULTS

Expectations were confirmed concerning the amount of change that would take place using the *PR*. Only 18.3% of the classification numbers were the same after reclassification. These were predominantly works with historical or geographical treatment

(780.9xx). The binomial proportion confidence interval for this statistic showed that with 90% confidence this proportion would be no more than ± 4% from the actual proportion in the UIUC Library. Thus at least the initial impact of implementing the *PR* would be great, because between 78% and 86% of all books would receive different classification numbers.

    To determine the most populous classes a frequency distribution of *DDC* 19 numbers was prepared (Table 1). Individual biography was the largest class of material in the sample. The next largest class was general music history. Ninety percent confidence intervals on these proportions were ± 9%. Most of the remainder of the sample contained fewer than three titles in each class number (141 class numbers, or 50% of the sample, each contained only one record). The ninety percent confidence interval on this proportion was ± 6%; thus between 44% and 56% of the books in the population can be expected to fall into classifications containing fewer than three titles.

Table 1: Most Populous Classes
DDC 19

Class Number	N	%	Subject
780.923	41	14.6	Individual biography
780.92	11	3.9	Individual biography
780.9	8	2.8	Historical & geographical treatment
781.57	6	2.1	Jazz
781.96	5	1.7	Librettoes
780.1	3	1.0	Philosophy and aesthetics
780.904	3	1.0	20th century music
781.15	3	1.0	Psychological principles
781.7291791	3	1.0	Ukranian music
782.1	3	1.0	Opera
782.109	3	1.0	Opera–Historical and geographical treatment
786.8054	3	1.0	Organ music

N = Number of sample books in *DDC* 19 class.

Among the reclassified records, individual biography was still
the most populous class (17.9%) (see Table 2). Thirty-nine records
fell among the specified composer numbers in class 789 and eleven
fell in the general classification (789 without subdivision). The next
most populous class was general music history (780.9). A ninety
percent confidence interval on this proportion was ± 9%. Of the
remaining class numbers, 188 (67%) occurred only once. The 90%
confidence interval for the unique numbers was ± 4.6%. Thus,
between 62.4% and 71.6% of books in the population classified using
the revised 780 can be expected to fall into classes containing only
one item. These distributions are illustrated in Table 2.

Table 2: Most Populous Classes
PR

Class Number	N	%	Subject
789	50	17.9	Composers
780.9	8	2.8	Historical & geographical treatment
780.278	5	1.7	Librettoes
780.92	4	1.4	Historical & geographical treatment–persons associated with music
780.77	3	1.0	Special teaching methods
780.904	3	1.0	20th century music
781.626	3	1.0	Jazz
782.10273	3	1.0	Operas–Printed music
782.109	3	1.0	Opera–Historical and geographical treatment

N = Number of sample books in *PR* class.

To ascertain the areas of the collection experiencing continued
growth (that is, topical areas in which books were being acquired), a
frequency distribution of *DDC* 19 classification numbers for all
works acquired after 1978 (the date of the retrospective shelflist
conversion) was constructed. Ninety-one of the 279 works in the

sample fell into this category (Table 3). Individual biography clearly predominated, but study and teaching, dramatic music, harmony, and general music history were also active classes. Of these, only the classification number for harmony had changed (from 781.3 in *DDC* 19 to 781.25 in the *PR*). Of these active classes, only individual biography and general music history correspond to the most populous classes noted above. Ninety percent confidence intervals for these proportions were wide, ranging from ±10% to ±16.7%, reflecting the fact that this group is a subset of a small sample. While the specific proportions in the population are likely to differ widely from those in the sample, it is still likely that these five classes remain those in which continued growth can be expected.

Table 3: Works Acquired After 1978

Class Number	N	%	Subject
780.92 ff	16	17.5	Individual biography
780.7 ff	6	6.5	Study and teaching
782.1 ff	4	4.3	Opera
781.3	3	3.2	Harmony
780.9	2	2.1	Historical and geographical treatment
ff.	60	65.9	Classes with 1 work apiece
	n = 91		

N = Number of sample books in *PR* class.

n = Total number of sample books in subset "acquired" after 1978.

Since it was clear that the majority of books were in topical areas for which classification numbers would not change, an interesting secondary problem was the degree of intermingling of topics that would occur in the less populous classes. The confidence intervals constructed for the proportions indicating dispersal among classes (50% under *DDC* 19 and 67% under the *PR*) were approximately ± 5%. These statistics indicate that with 90%

probability, between 45% and 55% of items were classed in unique numbers (that is, only one book appeared in each of these classes) under *DDC* 19, and that between 62% and 72% of items would be classed in unique numbers under the *PR*. Because large proportions of items would receive unique classification numbers, the disruptive effect of the implementation of the *PR* on browsing would be dependent to some extent on the degree to which newly classified works would be placed in classes that had represented different topics in *DDC* 19. Table 4 illustrates this effect. This table arrays the classification *numbers* that occurred in both *DDC* 19 and the *PR*. Few differences in meaning are observed.

Table 5 shows a few examples of books classified in numbers from the *PR* that will appear adjacent to the numbers from Table 4. Again, little intermingling of topics is observed.

Even though there appears to be little change for large classes of prolific materials, some groups of books will be placed in very different locations. For instance, works on musics of particular ethnic groups will be classed in 781.622ff. (subdivided by geographic area notation). These books were classed in 781.57 or 781.7 (with geographic subdivision) under *DDC* 19. Likewise, works on vocal music move from 784 to 782ff. This means that without reclassification, significant dislocation of these materials will occur.

An interesting comparison was the average length of the classification number in the successive editions of the schedule. In the UIUC Library's works classed using *DDC* 16, the average length was 5.13 digits. Using the 19th edition, the average length was 6.25 digits. In the *PR*, despite its increased use of faceting, the average length of the classification number was 7.2 digits. Ninety percent confidence intervals constructed for these means were $\pm$ .11, .17 and .23 respectively. A t-test of the difference observed between the means for *DDC* 19 and the *PR* indicated that the difference is statistically significant. Thus with 90% confidence it can be inferred that the average length of call numbers for books about music would increase slightly under the *PR*.

Table 4: Numbers that Occurred in Both Tests

	PR	DDC 19
780.1	Philosophy and theory	Philosophy and aesthetics
780.29	Commercial miscellany	Commercial miscellany
780.3	Dictionaries, ency., concord.	Dictionaries, ency., concord.
780.77	Special methods of teaching	Special methods of teaching
780.7974789	Festivals--Rochester, N.Y.	Festivals--Rochester, N.Y.
780.79773	Festivals--Illinois	Festivals--Illinois
780.9	Historical & geographical treatment	Historical & geographical treatment
780.902	History --500-1449 (medieval)	History --450-1850
780.9032	--1600-1750 (Baroque)	--1600-1750
780.9034	--1825-1900 (Romanticism)	--1825-1900
780.904	--20th century	--20th century
780.9040947	--20th century--USSR	--20th century--USSR
780.92	Persons associated with music	Persons associated with music
780.94212	Geographical treatment--London	Geographical treatment--London
780.943155	--Berlin	--Berlin
780.94352	--Bremen	--Bremen
780.946	--Spain	--Spain
780.94741	--Estonia	--Estonia
780.9485	--Sweden	--Sweden
780.9561	--Turkey & Cyprus	--Turkey & Cyprus
780.973	--U.S.	--U.S.
780.9755	--Virginia	--Virginia
781	General principles and forms	General principles & considerations
781.0903	--1450-	--Dictionaries, encyclopedias, concordances
781.15	Scientific principles	Psychological principles
781.2	Rudiments of music	Other basic considerations
781.207	Rudiments--Teaching methods	--Study and teaching
781.2077	Rudiments--Special methods	--Programmed texts
782.109	Opera--Historical & geographical treatment	Opera--Historical & geographical treatment
782.1092	Composers of opera	Persons associated with opera

Table 5: Adjacency

No Change	PR	Definitions
	780.0259794	Music and religion
780.1		Philosophy and esthetics
	780.148	--Musical notation
	780.2781	Words sung to music
780.29		Commercial miscellany
780.3		Dictionaries
	780.5	Serials
	780.7205	Study and teaching--Research--Periodicals
780.77		Special methods--Study & teaching
	780.77019	" --Psychological principles
	780.78	Performances
780.7974789		Festivals--Rochester, NY
	780.7975	Festivals--Southeastern U.S.
780.79773		Festivals--Illinois
780.92		Individual biography
	780.920903	--Modern period, 1500-
781		General Principles
	781.0902	Theory before renaissance
781.0903		Theory in renaissance
	781.11	Psychological principles
781.15		Scientific principles
	781.17	Artistic principles
781.2077		Rudiments--Special methods
	781.226	Rudiments-Meter
	782.077	Dramatic music--Ground bass
782.1		Opera
	782.10149	Dramatic music--Editing
	782.1071	Dramatic music--Schools
782.109		Opera--Historical and geographic treatment
	782.10903	"--1450-
782.1092		"--Composers, etc.
	782.140973	"--Plays, U.S.

Wajenberg has proposed a schema for machine manipulation and retrieval of *DDC* numbers.[16] He suggests a series of MARC codes using the currently undesignated second indicator of fields 082 and 092 in conjunction with a series of new subfields. In this way it would be possible to specify hierarchical relationships and, more to the point, the not readily apparent structure of synthesized numbers, so that the subfields could function as machine-readable facet indicators. For instance, Table 6 shows the range of numbers from the sample built to represent musics of various ethnic groups. Ukrainian folk music (781.62291791) is represented by 781.622 (for folk music) and 91791 (from *DDC* Table 5 for the Ukraine). The facet indicating the specific ethnic group, in this case the Ukraine, is not clearly delineated from the classification number for folk music. With machine-readable subfield coding the ethnic or geographic facets would be clearly delineated—and searchable.

Table 6: Synthetic Numbers*

781.62291791	Folk music/Ukrainians
781.6229181	Folk music/Bulgarians
781.6229187	Folk music/Slovaks
781.622942	Folk music/Mongols
781.62296073	Folk music/African-Americans
781.623098	Folk music/South Americans
781.6242	Western country music
781.626	Jazz
781.6263	Traditional jazz
781.6265	Modern jazz
781.6260166	Jazz/discography

*N.B.: These numbers were constructed using the *PR*.

The revised 780 specifically reserves two digits (0 and 1) for use in many places as facet indicators, so as to permit the user to specify and retrieve compound concepts contained in synthetic numbers. Wajenberg's scheme would significantly enhance the retrievability of all kinds of materials. For example, the numbers in Table 6 are highly synthetic. South American popular music (781.623098) consists of five parts—781 (Musical Forms), 6 (Traditions of music), 23 (Popular music), 09 (Standard subdivision for Geographical Treatment) and 8 (South America). In particular, the ability to retrieve by cultural group without specifying the terms used to build the base number could greatly enhance retrieval capability in online systems. For instance, if synthetic *DDC* numbers used subfield coding to indicate the various segments, searches for all music of Ukrainian character could be conducted.

Conclusions

The results of this study are necessarily limited. The confidence intervals constructed around the proportional measures for the active classes were wide, perhaps reflecting the low parameters used to design the study and indicating the chance that the real proportions might differ greatly in the collection. Nevertheless, it appears that in the main, intershelving of works classified using the *PR* would not create major disturbances for general collections of books about music. Most of the works in the sample fell into classes whose numbers were unique and thus would not conflict with other items. Many fell into classes whose numbers will not change or into hierarchical sequences that remain logical and comprehensible.

Hassell concluded that the *PR* would not appreciably improve retrieval or browsability of printed music among performers because of the dispersal of media caused by the use of form subdivisions, and because of its failure to properly subarrange both collections and

separates, and original works and arrangements. This conclusion is
not surprising in a classification that purports to serve as a
classification of knowledge rather than a pragmatic shelf-location
scheme for performance editions. Further, in a published response to
Hassell's article, Sweeney points out problems with Hassell's
preferred performance-oriented scheme (the basis of his tests), and
indicates the ease with which facet indicators can be employed to
achieve the desired subarrangements.[17]

Thus the prospects are good for the success of the revised 780.
The apparent advantages of the highly synthetic features of the *PR*,
demonstrated by the high dispersal of books among unique classes,
hold the promise of greatly enhanced retrieval ability for works of
music scholarship in online systems with a minimum of disruption
on the shelves.

Notes

1.   The authors wish to acknowledge the assistance of
William Grey Potter III, Elizabeth Fisher-Smith, and the UIUC
Library Research and Publication Committee. They also wish to
thank Gregory New, Decimal Classification Office, Libary of
Congress, for his assistance in acquiring a pre-print of the 780
schedule from the 20th edition.

2.   For a discussion of alternative schemes based on *DDC*, see
"Chapter 7: Classification," in Richard P. Smiraglia, *Music
Cataloging: The Bibliographic Control of Printed and Recorded
Music in Libraries* (Englewood, Colo.: Libraries Unlimited, 1989).

3.   *Proposed Revision of 780 Music: Based on Dewey Decimal
Classification and Relative Index*, prepared under the direction of
Russell Sweeney and John Clews (Albany, N.Y.: Forest Press, 1980).

4.   Geraint J. Philp, "The Proposed Revision of 780 Music and
Problems in the Development of Faceted Classification for Music,"
Brio 19 (Spring/Summer 1982): 1-13.

5.   Robert H. Hassell, "Revising the Dewey Music Schedules: Tradition vs. Innovation," *Library Resources & Technical Services* 26 (1982): 192.

6.   Ibid., 193.

7.   Ibid., 201.

8.   Ibid., 202; italics ours.

9.   Richard B. Wursten, "Review of *Proposed Revision of 780 Music*," *Cataloging and Classification Quarterly* 5, no. 2 (1984): 57.

10.   Philp, 11.

11.   These opinions and others were expressed in the documents considered by the American Library Association's Subcommittee to Review the Proposed Dewey 780 that was appointed by the Subject Analysis Committee of the Resources and Technical Services Division's Cataloging and Classification Section. Their final report was issued in Sept., 1984. Cf. [Frances Hinton], Chair, Subcommittee to Review the Proposed Dewey 780, memorandum to Peter Lisbon, Chair, Subject Analysis Committee, 18 Sept. 1984.

12.   Melvil Dewey, *Dewey Decimal Classification*. 20th ed. Albany: OCLC Forest Press, 1989. Vol. 4: *Manual*, pp. 205-206.

13.   An internal policy of the UIUC Library was to limit class number length to eleven digits.

14.   Diane Foxhill Carothers and William Aguilar, "The Beginnings of LCS at Illinois," *Information Technology and Libraries* 2 (Dec. 1983): 393-400.

15.   In anticipation of the twentieth edition of *DDC*, the Music Library announced in the spring of 1988 that it had decided to abandon Dewey Decimal classification of its book collection, preferring instead to use Library of Congress Classification. Cf. "News From the Music Library." (March, 1988).

16.   Arnold S. Wajenberg, "MARC Coding of DDC for Subject Retrieval," *Information Technology and Libraries* 2 (1983): 246-251.

17.   Russell Sweeney, "[Letter to the editor, *LRTS*, abridged]" *Library Resources & Technical Services* 27 (1983): 105-107.

A Music Muddle?
DDC 20 in the Public Library[1]
by
Pat Thomas

ABSTRACT: The implementation of *DDC* 20 and the revised 780 Music in a medium-sized public library is discussed, and the results of an *ad-hoc* study of the effects of the *Proposed Revision* ... on music and sound recordings are described. Practical suggestions for coping with the revision are given.

I'd like to share with you some thoughts about the cataloging of music in a public library. I've been cataloging for about 24 of the 37 years that I have spent as a professional librarian, and though I certainly don't claim to know it all, I've been around long enough to have observed a great deal, to have formed some opinions and to have made and corrected lots of mistakes.

Context: A Medium-Sized Public Library

First, let's talk about what is meant by a "medium-sized public library." I think my home base, the Stockton-San Joaquin County Public Library in California, is fairly typical. Stockton is a pleasant city located 78 miles inland, due east of San Francisco. The county is largely agricultural, but Stockton's deep water port serves as a shipping center for agricultural crops and manufactured products from the Central Valley of California as they move down through the Delta to San Francisco Bay and the Golden Gate. The community is exceptionally diverse, with many ethnic groups that have been

---

Pat Thomas is Head Cataloger, Stockton-San Joaquin County Public Library, Stockton, Calif.

represented throughout California's history, beginning with the
Spanish, the Chinese during the Gold Rush, later the Mexican
migrant workers, and most recently Southeast Asians in large
numbers. Stockton is the home of the University of the Pacific
(UOP), a small liberal arts college, with graduate schools of law,
dentistry and pharmacy. The University and the local community
college represent the only institutions of higher learning in the
county and offer the only other significant library resources to the
community. UOP has a fine conservatory and Stockton has a
symphony orchestra and a chorale, so music receives support.
However, the Public Library resources serve a community with
personal or amateur, rather than professional, interests in music; our
collection is general rather than specialized. The Public Library
serves the whole of San Joaquin County, with the exception of Lodi, a
small city next to the northern county line. We have a Central
Library and three smaller branches in the city of Stockton, six other
branches outside of the city limits (two of which, Manteca and Tracy,
serve small cities), and one very active bookmobile. The county
currently has a population of approximately 460,300 souls, of which
nearly 192,300 reside within the city of Stockton. The collection
consists of 267,000 titles and 1,289,828 volumes. We cataloged
21,000 titles and added 111,971 volumes in fiscal 1987/88; a staff of
120 administers a $5 million plus budget and circulated 1,696,811
items during that same fiscal year. So there you have it: a typical
medium-sized public library (if such a thing exists).

    Our collection consists of books, periodicals, scores, sheet
music, videos, records and audio-cassettes. We have not, as yet,
begun collecting CD's, though we hope to do so in the next fiscal year.
We have purchased an integrated automated system, with the
circulation and acquisitions modules currently up and running.
Retrospective conversion was done entirely on leased OCLC
terminals by temporary help and financed by a grant. We are now
negotiating a system upgrade, and when that is completed sometime
this fall, we will install additional terminals and introduce the public
access catalog to an unsuspecting public. We closed (that is, we

dumped) the card catalog in 1983, which was replaced with a COM (fiche) catalog produced from our OCLC archival tapes. All of our bibliographic records are in MARC format (thank heaven), though in order to get cross-references into the on-line system we will have a massive maintenance job ahead of us when authority control is added. We use the *Dewey Decimal Classification (DDC)*, and it is Library policy to adopt and implement a new edition of *DDC* when published. We do our cataloging using OCLC, though we also have the capability of creating MARC records on our local system. All of this verbiage so far is to acquaint you with a "typical medium-sized public library," with a typical catalog and typical cataloging procedures. I want to use it to give some perspective to a discussion of cataloging in general and music in particular.

Implementation of *DDC* 20

One important issue that needs to be addressed at this particular time is the implementation of the 20th edition of the *DDC*, which was published in February of 1989. As luck would have it, the major phoenix schedule published in this new edition is in music, the 780's. In 1980, the editors of *DDC* published a separate with the proposed new 780 classification. Given our classification policy of implementing new editions as they are published, we decided to test the workability of the new schedules. At that time, we had been spending most of our energy and resources on retrospective conversion. Consequently a large backlog had gathered. We browsed through this backlog and had no trouble finding a nice selection of materials quickly to use in our test. We classified 482 sound recordings, 128 titles of books about music, and 31 scores. We had cards printed, which we then filed in shelf list order to analyze what the new classification would do to the arrangement of materials in the collection. We didn't like what we found. As a result, I wrote letters and was asked to serve as a member of an RTSD Subject Analysis Committee (SAC) Subcommittee to Review the Proposed

Dewey 780. At that time (1984) the Subcommittee did a thorough study of the 780's phoenix schedule. Forest Press had solicited reactions to the proposed revision of 780 Music.[2] Our final report submitted changes that we felt were necessary to make the schedules work for mainstream libraries in the U.S. For example, the committee liked the idea of a list of composers, but felt that it did not offer a complete solution. We questioned why the list was limited to composers. For the generalist, such a list should probably be inclusive rather than exclusive, including performers, conductors, vocalists, musicians of all kinds, and possibly musical groups. We had used 780.92 for this purpose satisfactorily for years and saw no real advantage in the 789.9 as proposed. When it was proposed, the composers were limited to those names listed by the Decimal Classification Division of LC, which we felt was not inclusive enough, or up-to-date enough, to be useful. When asked, we expressed our preference for form first and executant secondary, especially in the vocal area. The human voice is much more difficult to classify precisely than is an instrument. An option was presented that suggested that 781-789.8 be used for only one tradition of music and all other traditions be classed in 789.9. The example given was for a folk music library, which would then use 789.9 for all other traditions,.e.g., jazz and "classical" music. This is a perfect example of the proposed revision favoring the special library over the general library for everyman.

The public library is, by definition, a general library. Indeed, some public libraries have fine special collections, but they are the exceptions to the rule. The biggest problem with the 780 phoenix for the public library is, of course, in the pop field, which is too big for us to ignore any longer, whether in sound recordings or in print materials; soon we will be unable to ignore music videos as well.

The Decimal Classification Division of LC attempted to answer some of the objections that were raised by the SAC Subcommittee in the final version of *DDC* 20. But I believe that they were too far committed to its adoption to make the changes that were really necessary to address the problems raised by the American public library community.

As the most widely used library classification system in the world, the *DDC* is the scheme of choice for 95% of the public and school libraries in the United States, as well as 25% of all college and university libraries, and 20% of all special libraries. According to the introduction of *DDC* 20,[3] it is used in more than 135 countries, and has been translated into over 30 languages. When I went to library school many years ago, there were also a large number of research and/or academic libraries who classified their collections using Dewey. Since that time many, though not all, of these larger library collections have been re-classed to the Library of Congress schedules. Such a trend would seem to indicate to me that Dewey lends itself better to a smaller, current, popular collection. Dewey's logical, hierarchical arrangement is particularly suitable for a collection available for browsing, and again, this is of no particular concern for a large, research collection with, in all probability, closed stacks. At any rate, to make my point, *DDC* has traditionally been a classification system for everyman, with provisions for extending numbers as necessary for closer, more specific notation, but intended as a means to arrange logically on the shelf a collection that represents the broad spectrum of man's knowledge. Speaking as a non-specialist in music, the phoenix schedule as it appears in *DDC* 20, is a scheme best suited to classify a predetermined collection with a known emphasis or bias. It is not meant for everyman's music collection wherever in the world such a collection might be found. It is particularly well suited to classify a large collection of scores with a strong emphasis on Western (European) classical music. It virtually assumes the user is a performer or an instrumentalist looking for some music to play or to perform. It does not, in my humble opinion, provide as well for a collection of sound recordings, which would seem to be more logically arranged first by musical form, then by performer or vocalist or instrument or composer.

As I indicated, I am not a specialist in music. I am fortunate; I have a knowledgeable staff member who catalogs the sound

recordings, scores and books about music that we add to the
collection. She is knowledgeable in the subject field of music and she
is knowledgeable in the MARC formats for the description of such
items. But that does not lessen my concern for others, particularly in
the public library field, for whom the new music schedule in *DDC* 20
does not provide a logical shelf arrangement for the variety of
materials that such libraries collect.

Perhaps you now understand what I mean when I say that the
new *DDC* 20 is not a subject to be taken lightly nor could a discussion
of its implementation be called fun. But that is not the whole truth.
On the whole the new Dewey is, I feel, a superior product. Given the
policy of implementation of a new edition of Dewey as published, this
preliminary dissatisfaction with the new 780's presents a dilemma. I
would never be one to recommend a huge recataloging project if I felt
that there was nothing to be gained by its accomplishment. True, we
are not satisfied with the music as classified according to *DDC* 19.
But we would gain nothing but a headache and heartburn if we went
to all the work to re-class. No improvement in shelf arrangement
would result.

Practical Suggestions for Coping

Keep in mind that I also want to present here some practical
suggestions on how to cope. Whenever I am in doubt about a solution
to a cataloging problem, I take to the phone! Surely someone else out
there in libraryland has the same or a similar problem. How are
some others coping? A number of questions came up as I chatted
with some of my colleagues around the country. Some had some
interesting things to say and perhaps presented a viewpoint that I
had never considered before. These conversations provided much
food for thought. But first, a disclaimer. The opinions that I am
about to share with you have absolutely no resemblance to a
scientific survey, and I make no bones about it. It was a "random"

sampling, all right, but they do not resemble research in its finest hour. They are interesting nonetheless.

First, very few medium-sized public libraries collect scores with any diligence. Some have collections, but few are actively collecting. I don't pretend to know what this means, except that few expressed enthusiasm for re-classifying a static collection. This situation describes our own collection of scores and sheet music. Another factor to consider is circulation. The music community in Stockton uses the collection though some of it is unclassified and very little of it is on-line. Frankly, we had been waiting for the new *DDC* 20 before we made a decision about how to classify or whether to re-classify it as we enter records on-line.

Let me pause here a moment to remind you that I keep referring to Stockton Public Library because I work there and I know our situation best. I am presenting it merely as a frame of reference. We don't know it all or have all the answers or even think that we have no problems. I certainly am not recommending that everyone do it our way. If that were true, I would never have called another soul to get an opinion or shared with you our dilemma about whether we should implement the new 780 schedule as published in *DDC* 20. The jury is still out on that one.

Let me digress again. It has been an assumption on our part for our library that in an integrated, automated system it would be desirable to classify all media by one scheme. If that were true, by doing a single call number search one would get all the materials in that classification number (that is, on the subject) that were in the collection. Take, for example, books and sound recordings for learning a language, which would be classed in the same number. Or, if one did a call number search for 796.352, one would retrieve both books and a video on golf. Or, if one did an appropriate call number search one could find books about Beethoven's Fifth as well as sound recordings, perhaps a video, etc., etc. I found that some do not share the opinion that it is desirable to give the same classification number to materials in all formats. In fact I heard more than once that to have one classification scheme for materials that are not shelved together can only be confusing. One library fiddled with the placement of the decimal in the Dewey classification number (not the numbers themselves) to make it look like a different classification system so that the patron would not think that the items were side by side on the shelf. I personally think it would take a pretty sophisticated user (or staff member for that matter) to recognize that device and to differentiate by that means one area of the collection from another.

Then, of course, there is the library out there that classifies everything according to Dewey, and that indeed interfiles everything, all formats, on the shelf. An interesting concept, which conjures up all kinds of interesting images. One worry would concern the selection of shelving. What kind would accommodate all formats? Does such an arrangement take up more space? Is that cost effective? How do the patrons like it? Do they want to find all the videos in one spot so they can see what you have? Does the staff like it? I'm just curious to know if it really works well.

Most of the libraries queried classified scores and sheet music in Dewey, as well as books about music. However, sound recordings were an entirely different matter. Most sound recording collections were classified in a totally different scheme. The name I heard most often was the $ANSCR^4$ system published in 1969, which offers quite a simple alternative to Dewey. The arrangement is quite attractive in that it approximates the arrangement I described above (first by musical form, then by performer or vocalist or instrument or composer). Other libraries had modified Dewey to suit their own local needs. If such was the case, however, that modification had been done several editions ago, so to speak. Other libraries had devised their own completely original system. In any of these instances, there is little incentive to change, even with the revised schedule in *DDC* 20. If it ain't broke, don't fix it.

Interestingly enough, I found total, universal agreement on one thing and one thing only. Everyone agreed that in this day of automation and local systems, everyone wanted a complete bibliographic description for all materials, regardless of format. Bah humbug to minimal level cataloging. In more than one case, public service staff had agreed that they only wanted minimal level cataloging, just to get it out on the shelf quickly. It wasn't long before they were back inquiring about those brief records. "They're useless!" I'm a great believer in the "do it once and do it right" school of cataloging practice. Quick and dirty never satisfies, and you pay dearly when you later enhance brief records.

It seems that very few libraries are buying records (i.e., lp's) currently. All you have to do is go to a record store to understand why. Audio cassettes and CD's are the runaway favorites. This might work to our advantage. In the public library the emphasis is on the here and now. If indeed we adopted the new 780's schedule now, in five years many of the records, cassettes and CD's currently in the collection would have dropped by the wayside and could then be weeded. There would always be that core of materials that time does not fade. Eventually one would have to re-classify, but by that time the project would be much smaller thanks to attrition.

Let me now share with you some random comments on a variety of aspects of this problem, the cataloging of music. These comments are in no particular order. (By now you might understand what I mean when I say my survey was strictly unscientific, and that refers to the results, too!)

1.   One library, which collects only audio tapes of the three formats available in sound recordings, uses *ANSCR* to classify those tapes because the library staff does not want the call number to resemble that of print materials. The song books in the collection are classified in Dewey and they will implement *DDC* "without looking back."

2.   Another library has a small collection of scores and sheet music classified in Dewey. The sound recordings collection, which includes CD's, audio tapes and records, is large and popular. The music portion of the sound recordings collection is classified using the *ANSCR* system. The staff

likes the *ANSCR* system, but the public finds one more classification system confusing. An interesting note about that particular collection concerns the spoken audio tapes (the "books on tape"). That portion of the collection is fully cataloged, but is not classified because *ANSCR* was not deemed appropriate. The materials, all 2,000 titles, are shelved separately in order by title. That case, to my way of thinking, presents a strong argument for classifying all materials in all formats according to the Dewey schedules. If such were the case, all manifestations of a title (print and audio recording, etc.) would be classified in the same number.

3.   A third library, with a sizable sound recordings collection, uses *ANSCR* because (and I quote) it is "not easy to use Dewey."

4.   The most often heard complaint about music in *DDC* 20 concerns the staff and their perception of the changes that its implementation will bring. Nearly every number is new. All the collective memory of staff members, dating back to the time when each of them went to library school and learned a few numbers from the Dewey schedules then in use, is going down the tube, falling into a black hole. If you adopt *DDC* 20 and you decide not to (or can't) re-class for whatever reason, the only solution offered is to split files. And then your problems begin. How do you indicate to the patron (or to the staff members for that matter) which file (which shelf) has a specific item? No logic there. How do you prevent a shelver from shelving the item in the wrong sequence? How do you know where to look?

5.   Then there is a library that had a grant to put their entire collection of song books on-line. These are the same books that the public service folks had so laboriously indexed on little 3-by-5 cards over the years, and which had never been classified before. And then we come to the terms of the grant. The idea was to put the entire table of contents on-line for

keyword searching as a substitute for the massive index. Of course, the grant was for last fiscal year. Never mind that a new Dewey was to hit the stands just the moment the project was completed. They had to spend their money and they couldn't wait. The collection had never before been classified. You guessed it! They had no choice but to classify the whole collection, which was sizable, using Dewey 19, and now they have a real dilemma. To re-class or not to re-class. That is the question.

6.   I can't verify this yet, but a number of folks with whom I talked were of the opinion that the notation was significantly longer using *DDC* 20. If your library policy limits call numbers to a certain number of digits after the decimal, it makes the whole classification process null and void. The resulting numbers are meaningless and serve no purpose.

Where Does this Leave Us?

Where does this leave us, folks? Well, I'm not sure that I know the answer to that question. One thing I do know is that the Library of Congress (LC) does not classify much that will help. These new schedules are not easy to apply. There is a whole new concept introduced in the 780's for number building. I am accustomed to using a 0 to add on to assigned numbers (e.g., when standard subdivisions are used), but in the 780's by using the digits 0 or 1 the classifier can show that a new facet is being introduced in the assigned number. This aspect of number building is unique to the schedules for music. For this reason it sends a warning signal to me. Does this signify the beginning of a trend? Over the years much of the usefulness of *DDC* has been dependent upon its simplicity for the classifier and for the end user. The introduction of the digit 1 as a facet indicator only in the 780's begins to gnaw away at the mnemonic features of *DDC* and the concept of uniformity across the schedules as a whole. Since the Decimal Classification Division of LC does not classify much in this field (sound recordings, music, etc.), they will not be able to assess the workability of the system as has been done traditionally in the past. Nor will LC's Dewey classifiers build a body of works classified and available on-line to serve as a guide to catalogers struggling to apply the new system correctly. I guess the ball is back in our court.

I am continually looking for some sort of meaning in life. Currently I'm looking for some sort of meaning in this music muddle. When *DDC* 20 was published and we received our copies in February, we made a preliminary study of the schedules as a whole including the changes that had been made in the 780's since the separate was published in 1980. We made the decision easily to adopt the new edition as a whole and began classifying right away in all areas except the 780's. We decided to delay a final decision in music until the dust settles. Since then I have talked to a number of librarians, and instead of dismissing the new schedule out of hand, we are trying to figure some way to make it work. I did speak to one individual who had some constructive ideas that we, the catalogers, could pursue if we feel strongly enough. I'm not trying to foment a revolution. I really am in favor of peaceful growth and change. Perhaps if some suggestions for alternative schemes could be published, we could devise our own solution. Or maybe more of us need to speak up and be heard with some constructive criticism for the classifiers/editors in the Decimal Classification Division of LC. One possibility would be an alternative classification number assigned according to a modified scheme, similar to the alternative number offered now in the fields of law and biography.

I would like to hear more discussion. It might be that further work could be done to find a solution for public libraries. I want to see, as well, how the numbers look in the abridged 12th edition of *DDC*, which is due to be published in late Spring 1990. If there are problems to be addressed they will be emphasized and magnified in the abridged edition. As I remarked earlier, the jury is still out. I personally am confident that a solution can be found if the 780's as published cannot be made to work for Everyman Public.

Notes

1.   This is a revision of a paper "Music in the Public Library," delivered at the 1989 American Library Association Annual Conference, Dallas, Texas, in a program session sponsored by the Public Library Association's Cataloging Needs of Public Libraries Committee.

2.   "Guidelines to Users for Reactions to *The Proposed Revision of 780 Music*," *DC&* 4 (Oct. 1981): 8-10.

3.   Melvil Dewey, *Dewey Decimal Classification and Relative Index*, 20th ed., ed. John P. Comaromi, et al. (Albany, N.Y.: Forest Press, 1989), xxvi.

4.   Caroline Saheb-Ettaba and Roger B. McFarland, *ANSCR: The Alpha-Numeric System for Classification of Recordings* (Williamsport, Pa.: Bro-Dart Publishing Co., 1969).

Bibliography

by

Richard B. Wursten

Bentley, Paul. "The Dewey Decimal Classification and Music." *Cataloguing Australia* 6 (July-Sept. 1980): 27-42.

Berman, Sanford. *HCL Cataloging Bulletin,* no. 36 (Sept./Oct. 1978): 1-47.

Bryant, Eric T., *Music Librarianship: A Practical Guide.* London: James Clarke & Co., 1959.

Bryant, Eric T., and Guy A. Marco. *Music Librarianship: A Practical Guide,* 2d ed. Metuchen, N.J.: Scarecrow Press, 1985.

Clews, John P., "The Revision of DC 780–The 'Phoenix' Schedule." *Brio* 12 (Spring 1975): 7-14.

Coates, E. J., comp. *British Catalogue of Music Classification.* London: British National Bibliography, 1960.

Comaromi, John P. "Dewey in the USA and Canada." *Catalogue & Index* 43 (Winter 1976): 3-5.

Dewey, Melvil. *A Classification and Subject Index for Cataloguing and Arranging the Books and Pamphlets of a Library.* Amherst, Mass., 1876.

--------------. *Decimal Classification and Relativ Index.* 11th ed., revised and enlarjd. Lake Placid Club, Adirondaks, N.Y.: Forest Pres, 1922.

--------------. *Decimal Classification and Relativ Index.* 12th ed., revised and enlarjd under direction of Dorcas Fellows. Lake Placid Club, Essex, N.Y.: Forest Pres, 1927.

--------------. *Decimal Classification.* 15th ed. Lake Placid Club, N.Y.: Forest Press, 1951.

---------------. *Decimal Classification and Relative Index.* 16th ed.,
      Lake Placid Club, Essex Co., N.Y.: Forest Press, 1958.
---------------. *Dewey Decimal Classification and Relative Index,*
      19th ed., ed. Benjamin A. Custer. Albany, N.Y.: Forest Press,
      1979.
---------------. *Dewey Decimal Classification and Relative Index.*
      Edited by John P. Comaromi, Julianne Beall, Winton E.
      Matthews, Jr., Gregory R. New. Albany, N.Y.: Forest Press,
      1989.
Forrest, Charles and Richard P. Smiraglia. "Radical Change with
      Minimal Disruption: The Effect of Revised 780 Music on the
      University of Illinois Library Shelf Arrangement." In *In
      Celebration of Revised 780*, comp. by Richard B. Wursten.
      MLA Technical Report no. 19. Canton, MA: Music Library
      Association, 1990, pp. 60-77.
Guidelines to Users for Reactions to the *Proposed Revision of 780
      Music," DC&* 4 (Oct. 1981): 8-10.
Hassell, Robert H. "Revising the Dewey Music Schedules:
      Tradition vs. Innovation." *Library Resources & Technical
      Services* 26 (1982): 192-203.
Hornbostel, Erich M. von, and Curt Sachs. "Classification of Musical
      Instruments." Translated by Anthony Baines and Klaus P.
      Wachsmann, *Galpin Society Journal* 14 (1961): 3-29.
McColvin, Lionel Roy, and Harold Reeves. *Music Libraries: Their
      Organization and Contents.* 2 vols. London: Grafton, 1937.
---------------. *Music Libraries: Their Organization and Contents.* 2
      vols. Completely rewritten, revised and extended by Jack
      Dove. London: Deutsch, 1965.
Manual on the Use of the Dewey Decimal Classification: Edition 19.
      Prepared by John P. Comaromi and Margaret J. Warren.
      Albany, N.Y.: Forest Press, 1982.
Matthews, Winton E., Jr. "Appreciation of 780 Music; or, Left-
      Handed Bell Ringing." In *In Celebration of Revised 780*, comp.
      by Richard B. Wursten. MLA Technical Report no. 19.
      Canton, MA: Music Library Association, 1990, pp. 39-52.

Meyer-Baer, Kathi. "Classifications in American Music Libraries."
    In *Reader in Music Librarianship*. Edited by Carole June
    Bradley. Westport, Conn.: Greenwood Press, 1973, pp. 172-
    76.

Music Library Association. Working Group on Access via Medium
    of Performance. "Proposed Revision of MARC Field 048"
    (Preliminary Draft, February 1983 [Revised: January 1984]
    (Photocopy).

Philp, Geraint J. "The Proposed Revision of 780 Music and
    Problems in the Development of Faceted Classification for
    Music." *Brio* 19 (Spring/Summer 1982): 1-13.

*Proposed Revision of 780 Music: Based on Dewey Decimal
    Classification and Relative Index*. Prepared under the
    direction of Russell Sweeney and John Clews. Albany, N.Y.:
    Forest Press, 1980.

Redfern, Brian. *Organizing Music in Libraries*. Revised ed. 2 vols.
    London: Clive Bingley; Hamden, Conn.: Linnet Books, 1978.

Saheb-Ettaba, Caroline, and Roger B. McFarland. *ANSCR: The
    Alpha-Numeric System for Classification of Recordings*.
    Williamsport, Pa.: Bro-Dart Publishing Co., 1969.

Stevenson, Gordon. "Classification Chaos." In *Reader in Music
    Librarianship*. Edited by Carole June Bradley. Westport,
    Conn.: Greenwood Press, 1973, pp. 274-78.

Sweeney, Russell. "Grand Messe des 780's (With Apologies to
    Berlioz)." In *In Celebration of Revised 780*, comp. by Richard
    B. Wursten. MLA Technical Report no. 19. Canton, MA:
    Music Library Association, 1990, pp. 28-38.

---------------. "Music in the Dewey Decimal Classification," *Catalogue
& Index*, 42 (Autumn 1976): 4-6.

---------------. "The Proposed Revision of 780 Music ... A reply."
    Brio 19 (Autumn/Winter 1982): 47-49.

---------------. (Response to Robert H. Hassell). *Library Resources &
    Technical Services* 27 (1983): 105-7.

Thomas, Pat. "A Music Muddle? Music in the Public Library," In
        In Celebration of Revised 780, comp. by Richard B. Wursten.
        MLA Technical Report no. 19. Canton, MA: Music Library
        Association, 1990, pp. 78-90.

Wajenberg, Arnold S. "MARC Coding of *DDC* for Subject Retrieval."
        Information Technology and Libraries 2 (Sept. 1983): 246-251.

----------------. "Online Subject Retrieval Using the New Schedule." In
        In Celebration of Revised 780, comp. by Richard B. Wursten.
        MLA Technical Report no. 19. Canton, MA: Music Library
        Association, 1990, pp. 53-59.

Wells, Arthur J., ed. *The British Catalogue of Music*. London: The
        Council of the British National Bibliography, 1975-   .

Wursten, Richard B. "Review of Proposed Revision of 780 Music."
        Cataloging & Classification Quarterly 5 (Winter 1984): 57-66.

Appendix: Two-Level Summmary of 780, *DDC* 20

780.000 1-.099 9   Relation of music to other subjects
　　.1-.9   Standard subdivisions

781   General principles and musical forms
　　.01-.09   Standard subdivisions
　　.1   Basic principles
　　.2   Elements of music
　　.3   Composition
　　.4   Techniques of music
　　.5   Kinds of music
　　.6   Traditions of music
　　.7   Sacred music
　　.8   Musical forms

782   Vocal music
　　.001-.009   Standard subdivisions
　　.01-.08   [General principles and musical forms]
　　.1   Dramatic vocal forms   Operas
　　.2   Nondramatic vocal forms
　　.3   Services (Liturgy and ritual)
　　.4   Secular forms
　　.5   Mixed voices
　　.6   Women's voices
　　.7   Children's voices
　　.8   Men's voices
　　.9   Other types of voices

783   Music for single voices   The voice
　　.001-.009   Standard subdivisions
　　.01-.09   [General principles and musical forms]
　　.1   Single voices in combination
　　.2   Solo voice
　　.3   High voice
　　.4   Middle voice
　　.5   Low voice
　　.6-.8   Woman's, child's, man's voice
　　.9   Other types of voices

784   Instruments and instrumental ensembles and their music
.01-.09   Standard subdivisions
.1   General principles, musical forms, instruments
.2   Full (Symphony) orchestra
.3   Chamber orchestra
.4   Light orchestra
.6   Keyboard, mechanical, electronic, percussion bands
.7   String orchestra
.8   Wind band
.9   Brass band

785   Ensembles with only one instrument per part
.001-.009   Standard subdivisions
.01-.08   [General principles, musical forms, instruments]
.1   Ensembles by size
.2   Ensembles with keyboard
.3   Ensembles without electrophones and with percussion and keyboard
.4   Ensembles without keyboard
.5   Ensembles without keyboard and with percussion
.6   Keyboard, electrophone, percussion ensembles
.7   String ensembles   Bowed string ensembles
.8   Woodwind ensembles
.9   Brass ensembles

786   Keyboard, mechanical, electrophonic, percussion instruments
.2   Pianos
.3   Clavichords
.4   Harpsichords
.5   Keyboard wind instruments Organs
.6   Mechanical and aeolian instruments
.7   Electrophones   Electronic instruments
.8   Percussion instruments
.9   Drums and devices used for percussion effects

787   Stringed instruments (Chordophones)
        Bowed stringed instruments
  .2   Violins
  .3   Violas
  .4   Cellos (Violincellos)
  .5   Double basses
  .6   Other bowed stringed instruments Viols
  .7   Plectral instruments
  .8   Plectral lute family
  .9   Harps and musical bows

788   Wind instruments (Aerophones)
  .2   Woodwind instruments and free aerophones
  .3   Flute family
  .4   Reed instruments
  .5   Double-reed instruments
  .6   Single-reed instruments
  .7   Saxophones
  .8   Free reeds
  .9   Brass instruments (Lip-reed instruments)

(789)   Composers and traditions of music

MLA Technical Reports

A Music Library Association *Technical Report* should help to
fill the gap between formal scholarly books and journals, and less
rigorous communication channels such as newsletters.

Because it can be prepared and disseminated with
comparative speed, a technical report is the most suitable vehicle for
the facile communication of research results or technical
developments in music librarianship. Consequently, the series
encompasses a wide variety of informational reports in a wide
variety of communication formats.

Manuscripts should be submitted to Richard P. Smiraglia,
Editor, MLA Technical Reports, 4416 Locust Street, Philadelphia,
PA 19104. Manuscripts should be double-spaced throughout,
typewritten or printed in correspondence or near letter quality mode
with a computer printer on one side of 8½ x 11 inch bond paper. They
should conform to the style guidelines of *The Chicago Manual of
Style*, 13th edition, revised (Chicago: University of Chicago Press,
1982).

MLA Technical Reports

1.   SLACC, the Partial Use of the Shelf List as Classed Catalog, by Donald Seibert, 1973.

2.   Directory of Music Library Automation Projects, by Garret H. Bowles. Rev. ed., 1989.

7.   Shelving Capacity in the Music Library, by Robert Michael Fling, 1981.

9.   Shelflisting Music: Guidlines for Use with the Library of Congress Classification: M, by Richard P. Smiraglia, 1981.

11.   The Acquisition and Cataloging of Music and Sound Recordings: A Glossary, compiled by Suzanne E. Thorin and Carole Franklin Vidali, 1984.

13.   The MARC Music Format from Inception to Publication, by Donald Seibert, 1983.

15.   Sheet Music Cataloging and Processing: a Manual, by Sarah J. Shaw and Lauralee Shiere, 1984.

16.   Authority Control in Music Libraries, Proceedings of the Music Library Association Preconference, March 5, 1985, edited by Ruth Tucker, 1989.

17.   Planning and Caring for Library Audio Facilities, edited and with a preface by James P. Cassaro, 1989.

18.   Careers in Music Librarianship, compiled by Carol Tatian, 1990.

19.   In Celebration of Revised 780: Music in the Dewey Decimal Classification Edition 20, compiled by Richard B. Wursten, 1990.